Wonderful ways to prepare

# CHINESE MEALS

## by LESLIE PROW

edited by MARION MANSFIELD

STEAMED PORK RICE BALLS (RECIPE PAGE 21)

Wonderful ways to prepare

# CHINESE
# MEALS

H.C. PUBLISHING INC.
FLORIDA, USA

COVER PICTURE — SEE PAGES 23 and 60

FIRST PUBLISHED 1979
REPRINTED 1984
FIRST US EDITION 1984

PUBLISHED AND COPYRIGHT © 1979
BY AYERS & JAMES
CROWS NEST, N.S.W., AUSTRALIA

DISTRIBUTED BY
AYERS & JAMES, CROWS NEST, N.S.W., AUSTRALIA
H.C. PUBLISHING INC., U.S.A.

PRINTED IN SINGAPORE

HARD COVER EDITION: ISBN 0 87637 928 5
SOFT COVER EDITION: ISBN 0 87637 940 4

TITLES AVAILABLE IN THIS SERIES: BEEF,
FISH & SEAFOOD, POULTRY, STEWS & CASSEROLES,
BARBECUES & PICNIC MEALS, CHINESE MEALS,
SALADS, SOUPS, ITALIAN MEALS, LAMB,
CAKES & COOKIES, DESSERTS.

◄ OVERLEAF — BANQUET LOBSTER (RECIPE PAGE 28)   STIR-FRIED PRAWNS AND VEGETABLES (RECIPE PAGE 28) ►

# Beef with Watercress

Serves: 4–6
Cooking time: 10–12 minutes

1½ lbs (750 g) lean beef
3 tablespoons soy sauce
3 tablespoons dry sherry
1 teaspoon sugar
½ teaspoon sesame oil
1 bunch watercress or 4 leaves of spinach
4 leeks
¾ lb (375 g) fresh mushrooms
8 oz (230 g) can bamboo shoots
½ lb (250 g) bean sprouts
1 teaspoon cornstarch
¼ cup chicken stock
6 tablespoons oil
½ teaspoon glutamate
Vermicelli — Transparent Noodles — see recipe
   page 32

Remove all fat and sinew from meat, cut into ¼" (5 mm) thin slices and then in half, place in a bowl with soy sauce, sherry, sugar and sesame oil and mix well. Cover bowl and chill for 2 hours. Wash watercress, chop leeks into slices and clean and halve the mushrooms. Drain bamboo shoots and cut into thin slices, drain bean sprouts and blend cornstarch with stock.

Heat 2 tablespoons of oil in a wok or pan, until very hot, add a quarter of the meat and stir-fry for 1 minute, until brown, then remove from wok, stir-fry remaining meat in batches. Heat remaining oil in the wok, add leeks and mushrooms and stir-fry for 2 minutes. Return all the meat to the wok with bamboo shoots and cornstarch stock and stir until mixture is boiling. Add glutamate, watercress and bean sprouts and stir-fry for 2 minutes or until watercress is wilted. Serve immediately with the noodles.

MONOGOLIAN LAMB WITH BELL PEPPER (RECIPE PAGE 25) ▶

## Short or Wonton Soup

Serves: 4
Cooking time: 15–18 minutes

¼ lb (125 g) ground pork
¼ lb (125 g) shrimp, finely chopped
1 thin slice root ginger, crushed
1 tablespoon soy sauce
½ teaspoon salt
1 clove garlic, crushed
few drops of sesame oil
16 Wonton Wrappers, see recipe page 63
1 egg, lightly beaten
boiling salted water
4 cups (1 liter) chicken stock
2 scallions, finely cut

Combine pork, prawns, ginger, soy sauce, salt garlic and sesame oil in a bowl and mix well. Place a teaspoon of the mixture slightly below center of a wonton wrapper and brush the edges of the wrapper with egg. Fold wrapper in half to make a triangle and press edges to seal, excluding any air. Moisten the two edges of the triangle with egg, bring together and pinch to seal. Drop wonton into boiling salted water and cook for 10 minutes. Meanwhile, bring chicken stock to the boil in a pan, reduce heat and simmer for 2–3 minutes. Lift out wonton, place 4 in individual bowls and add the chicken stock, garnish with chopped scallions and serve.

## Beef and Tomato Soup

Serves: 6
Cooking time: 30–35 minutes

1½ lbs (375 g) cooked soup bone
1½ tablespoons oil
1 medium onion, chopped
3 cups (750 ml) beef stock
5 medium tomatoes, peeled and chopped
pinch of salt
black pepper
¼ teaspoon five spice powder
½ cup (125 ml) tomato purée
chopped parsley for garnish

Chop meat from the bone into bite size pieces. Heat the oil in a wok or pan, add onion and stir-fry until transparent, add beef stock, bring to the boil, cover and simmer for 5 minutes. Add beef, tomatoes, salt, black pepper, five spice powder and tomato purée, return to the boil, cover and simmer for 20 minutes. Serve garnished with chopped parsley.

MARINATED PORK (RECIPE PAGE 24) ▶

# Beef Canton Style

Serves: 4–6
Cooking time: 8–10 minutes

1 lb (500 g) rump or topround steak
3 teaspoons cornstarch
6 tablespoons soy sauce
2 green bell peppers
1 red bell pepper
2 red chillies
2 scallions
½ cup (125 ml) oil
1 clove garlic, crushed
2 thin slices fresh root ginger, crushed
½ teaspoon salt
1 teaspoon sugar
pinch of glutamate
3 tablespoons dry white wine
Boiled or Fluffy Rice — see recipes pages 86 &
  37

Cut meat into long thin slices and place in a bowl, sprinkle with cornstarch and 2 tablespoons soy sauce and allow to stand for 5 minutes. Wash and seed the bell peppers and chillies and cut into thin slices. Cut scallions into 2″ (5 cm) lengths.

Heat half the oil in a wok or pan, add garlic, ginger and scallions and stir-fry for 1 minute, add bell peppers and chillies, sprinkle with salt and cook, stirring, for 2 minutes, then remove from the wok and set aside.

Add remaining oil to the wok and heat, add meat mixture and sauté over high heat for 1–2 minutes, until very lightly browned. Return pepper mixture to the wok, add remaining soy sauce, sugar, glutamate and wine and stir-fry for 1 minute. Serve immediately with rice.

DELUXE LEMON CHICKEN (RECIPE PAGE 25) ▶

# Rump Steak with Cashews

Serves: 4
Cooking time: 10–12 minutes

1 lb (500 g) rump steak
8 oz (230 g) can bamboo shoots
½ cup (125 ml) chicken stock
1 teaspoon satay sauce
1 teaspoon sesame oil
2 teaspoons soy sauce
1½ tablespoons cornstarch
1 tablespoon dry sherry
4 tablespoons peanut oil
1 clove garlic, crushed
1 slice ginger root, crushed
½ cup peas, fresh or frozen
¾ cup unsalted cashew nuts

Discard any fat from meat and slice into ¼″ (5 mm) strips, cut strips into 2″ (5 cm) pieces. Drain bamboo shoots and cut into small wedges. Combine stock, satay sauce, sesame oil and soy sauce in a bowl, blend cornstarch with sherry and add, stirring well and set aside for the sauce mixture.

Heat 2 tablespoons of oil in a wok or pan, add garlic and ginger and stir-fry for 1 minute, add the meat and sauté 1–2 minutes, until lightly browned, then lift out meat and drain on paper towels. Add remaining oil to the wok and heat, add bamboo shoots and stir-fry for 1 minute, add sauce mixture, peas and cashews and bring to the boil, reduce heat and simmer for 2 minutes. Return meat to the wok and simmer for 1 minute. Serve immediately on warm plates.

12

CHINESE PANCAKES AND PEKING DUCK (RECIPES PAGE 20) ▶

# Kowloon Fried Rice

Serves: 4
Cooking time: 8–10 minutes

> ½ lb (250 g) pork flank
> 6 oz (200 g) can Chinese sausage
> ½ red bell pepper sliced
> 2 eggs, beaten
> 4 tablespoons oil
> 3 cups cooked rice, drained and cooled
> 2 tablespoons soy sauce
> pinch of pepper
> 1 teaspoon salt

Discard rind from pork and dice. Drain and slice sausages. Beat the eggs well. Heat 1 tablespoon of oil in a wok or pan, pour in eggs and cook, do not stir, 1–2 minutes, lift out egg, slice and set aside. Heat remaining oil, add pork and sausage and stir-fry for 2 minutes, lift out and drain. Re-heat oil, add rice and soy sauce and cook for 1 minute, stirring constantly to keep grains separated. Return pork and sausage to the wok, add bell pepper, pepper and salt and stir-fry for 2 minutes, add egg slices, stir and serve.

# Egg Drop Soup

Serves: 4
Cooking time: 8–10 minutes

> ½ lb (250 g) cooked chicken meat
> 3 scallions, finely chopped
> 2 eggs
> 1 teaspoon water
> 5 cups (1 ¼ liters) chicken stock
> ½ teaspoon sugar
> ½ teaspoon salt
> ¼ teaspoon sesame oil
> finely chopped parsley

Finely chop or mince the chicken. Beat eggs and water in a bowl. Bring the stock to the boil in a large pan; reduce heat to a simmer, stir in sugar, salt, sesame oil and chicken meat and cook gently for 2 minutes. Stirring, slowly pour in the beaten eggs to form thin threads. Add scallions and remove pan from heat. Leave for ½ a minute, then serve sprinkled with parsley.
If a thick soup is preferred, thicken liquid with 1 tablespoon of cornstarch blended with 2 tablespoons water. Add cornstarch before the eggs and stir until soup thickens.

SPRING ROLLS (RECIPE PAGE 29) ▶

# Prawn Cutlets

Serves: 4
Cooking time: 8−10 minutes

1 lb (500 g) fresh prawns
3 teaspoons light soy sauce
½ teaspoon salt
1 tablespoon sherry
pinch of glutamate
1 egg, beaten
dry breadcrumbs
oil for cooking
lemon wedges
Plum Sauce — see recipe page 89

Shell and de-vein prawns, leaving tails intact. Cut through the back of each prawn and flatten out with the hand. Mix soy sauce, salt, sherry and glutamate in a dish, add prawns and marinate for at least 1 hour, basting often, until marinade is absorbed. Dip prawns in egg and cover with breadcrumbs, pressing in well. Cook in a deep pan of hot oil until golden brown, drain on paper towels and serve hot, with lemon wedges and Plum Sauce. (Illustrated above.)

# Dim Sims – Wun Tun

Serves: 8–10
Cooking time: 20–25 minutes

½ lb (250 g) ground pork
¼ lb (125 g) finely chopped prawns or shrimp
1 egg
3 scallions, finely chopped
3 dried mushrooms, soaked and chopped
½ cup shredded Chinese cabbage
pinch of glutamate
½ teaspoon salt
1 teaspoon sugar
3 teaspoons soy sauce
1 teaspoon sesame oil
40–45 Wonton Wrappers — see recipe page 63

Combine pork, prawns, egg, scallions, mushrooms, cabbage, glutamate, salt, sugar, soy sauce and sesame oil in a bowl and mix well. Place a teaspoon of the mixture in the center of each wrapper. Crease the wrapper as it is smoothed around the filling, leaving the tops free.
Lightly oil a large steamer and arrange dim sims, upright, in a single layer, cover tightly and steam over boiling water for 20–25 minutes. Lift out and serve hot or cold with a dipping sauce.
Or, lower dim sims into a deep pan of hot oil and cook for 4–5 minutes, until golden brown. Drain and serve.
*(Illustrated on opposite page.)*

# Three Story Prawns

Serves: 4
Cooking time: 12–15 minutes

1 lb (500 g) fresh prawns
thick slices of bread
1 egg, lightly beaten
2 tablespoons cornstarch
pinch of salt
1 slice of ham
1 scallion
oil for cooking

Shell and de-vein prawns and gently flatten. Toast the bread lightly, discard crusts and cut each slice into three fingers. Mix beaten egg, cornstarch and salt together in a bowl, add prawns and baste to cover. Cut the ham into small squares and cut scallion into ½″ (1 cm) lengths.
Place a prawn on each finger of toast and top with a little ham and scallion, spread a little of remaining cornstarch mixture on top and smooth to adhere to toast. Heat oil in a wok or pan, add toast fingers, with topping facing down, and cook for 4–5 minutes, until golden brown, turn fingers and lightly brown. Lift out and drain on paper towels. Serve hot with a dipping sauce.
*(Illustrated on opposite page.)*

# Deep Fried Squid

Serves: 4
Cooking time: 8–10 minutes

1 lb (500 g) baby squid
salted water
flour
salt and pepper
oil for deep frying
lemon wedges
Sweet and Sour Sauce — see recipe page 90

**Batter:**
2 tablespoons self-raising flour
½ teaspoon salt
¼ teaspoon baking soda
1 egg
2 tablespoons water

To make the batter, sift flour, salt and soda into a bowl and add the egg, gradually stir in the water and mix to a smooth batter.
Wash and clean the squid and cut into 3″ (7½ cm) pieces, slash the inside flesh with a sharp knife in a diamond pattern. Place squid in a pan with salted water and boil for 2 minutes. Lift out, drain and pat dry, then roll in flour, seasoned with salt and pepper. Dip squid into batter and cook in a deep pan of hot oil for 4–5 minutes, until golden brown. Lift out, drain on paper towels and serve with Sweet and Sour Sauce, garnish with lemon wedges.
*(Illustrated on opposite page.)*

# Scallop Balls

Serves: 4–6
Cooking time: 12–15 minutes

12 scallops
1 lb (500 g) fresh prawns or shrimp
4 scallions
½ teaspoon salt
½ teaspoon sugar
½ teaspoon glutamate
1 teaspoon cornstarch
½ teaspoon peanut oil
extra cornstarch
oil for deep frying
Sweet and Sour Sauce — see recipe page 90

**Batter:**
1 cup self-raising flour
½ teaspoon baking soda
½ teaspoon salt
1 cup (250 ml) water

To prepare batter, sift flour, soda and salt into a bowl and gradually stir in water. Mix to a smooth batter and set aside.

Wash scallops and pat dry. Shell and de-vein prawns and chop very finely or mince. Wash and finely chop scallions. Combine prawn mince, scallions, salt, sugar, glutamate, cornstarch and peanut oil in a dish and mix well, then divide mixture into 12 portions. Coat each scallop with a portion of prawn mixture to seal and make balls and dust with extra cornstarch. Place each ball on a fork, dip in batter, then slip into deep hot oil, 4 at a time, and cook for 3–4 minutes, until golden brown, then drain and keep warm. Do not have oil overhot. Serve hot with the sauce poured over balls.

CREAMED PRAWN SOUP (RECIPE PAGE 20) ▶

# Creamed Prawn Soup

Serves:   4–6
Cooking time:   8–10 minutes

  ¼ lb (125 g) shelled baby prawns, or shrimp
  1 cup desiccated coconut
  2 cups (500 ml) milk
  2 slices of bread for croutons
  2 cups (500 ml) heavy cream
  pinch of salt
  ½ teaspoon glutamate
  3 peppercorns, crushed
  1 medium onion, finely chopped
  1 clove garlic, crushed
  1 teaspoon soy sauce
  1 tablespoon sugar
  juice of 1 lemon

Combine coconut and milk in a pan and heat until tepid, remove from heat and set aside for 35–40 minutes. Toast bread slices, discard crusts, cut into small squares and keep warm.

To the coconut milk, add cream, salt, glutamate, prawns, peppercorns, onion, garlic, soy sauce and sugar and slowly bring to the boil, stirring occasionally. Reduce heat and simmer for 4–5 minutes, add lemon juice and stir. Serve hot with croutons.
*(Illustrated on page 19.)*

# Peking Duck

Serves:   6–8
Cooking time:   1½–1¾ hours
Oven:   220°C reduce to 190°C increase to 280°C
          425°F reduce to 375°F increase to 500°F

  5 lbs (2½ kg) dressed duck
  ½ teaspoon ground cinnamon
  2 thin slices green ginger, crushed
  ¼ teaspoon ground nutmeg
  ¼ teaspoon white pepper
  ¼ teaspoon ground cloves
  1 tablespoon soy sauce
  1 tablespoon honey
  4 scallions, cut in thin slices
  Chinese Pancakes — see recipe this page
  Plum Sauce — see recipe page 89

Rinse duck thoroughly, pat dry with paper towels and remove neck and giblets. Mix cinnamon, ginger, nutmeg, pepper and cloves together. Dust the inside of the duck with ½ spoonful of the spice mixture and rub remainder over the outside of the bird. Close the cavity with skewers, wrap duck tightly in foil to seal and chill for 12 hours or overnight.

Place wrapped duck in a baking dish and cook in a very hot oven for 1 hour, remove dish and allow duck to stand for 15 minutes. Reduce oven heat to moderately hot. Carefully open foil at one end, drain juices and fat into a bowl, then discard foil, and prick the duck skin all over with a fork. Place a rack in the pan, return duck to the oven and cook for 30 minutes.

Blend soy sauce with honey and brush liberally over the duck. Raise oven heat to extra hot and cook to glaze and brown duck for 4–5 minutes, but do not burn. Remove duck and with a sharp knife remove skin carefully and cut into pieces. Carve the duck and place on a warm platter with the glazed skin, sprinkle with scallions and serve with pancakes and Plum Sauce.
*(Illustrated on page 13.)*

# Chinese Pancakes

Serves:   6–8
Cooking time:   15 minutes

  3 cups flour
  1 teaspoon salt
  1 cup (250 ml) boiling water
  1½ tablespoons oil or sesame oil

Mix flour and salt in a bowl, gradually stir in boiling water with a wooden spoon, and mix until smooth, then set aside for 25–30 minutes. Form dough into a long 2″ (5 cm) roll and cut into ½″ (1 cm) rounds. Roll rounds into balls, then flatten to ¼″ (5 mm) round cakes. Brush cakes lightly, with oil, dust with flour and roll out into very thin pancakes.

Cook in a pan, one at a time, over low heat, turning once, until slightly bubbly and starting to curl. Lift out, stack and cover with a damp cloth, until required.

With Peking Duck, place a small amount of the duck and glazed skin on pancake, sprinkle with scallions, add Plum Sauce or Bean Paste Jam, roll up and eat with fingers.
*(Illustrated on page 13.)*

# Eggplant Soup

Serves:  4–6
Cooking time:  20–25 minutes

　2 eggplants
　1 medium onion
　2 scallions
　2 teaspoons peanut oil
　1 small clove garlic, crushed
　4 cups (1 liter) chicken stock
　¼ teaspoon salt
　¼ teaspoon pepper
　2 drops Tabasco sauce
　¼ teaspoon thyme
　½ cup (125 ml) heavy cream

Wash and peel eggplants and cut into cubes. Peel and chop onion finely. Wash scallions and chop finely. Heat the oil in a large pan, add eggplant, garlic, onion and scallions and sauté for 1–2 minutes. Add stock, salt, pepper, Tabasco and thyme, cover and simmer gently for 15 minutes. Remove pan from heat and allow to cool slightly, then put through a blender to purée, or beat well. Stir in cream, heat to hot, but not boiling, and serve.

# Garlic Prawns

Serves:  4
Cooking time:  12–15 minutes

　1 lb (500 g) prawns or shrimp
　1 onion
　2 tablespoons soy bean paste
　2 tablespoons dry sherry
　salt and pepper to taste
　1 tablespoon cornstarch
　water
　oil for deep cooking
　1 tablespoon peanut oil
　6 cloves garlic, crushed
　Fried Rice — see recipe page 66

Retaining tails, shell and de-vein prawns, rinse and pat dry. Peel onion and chop finely. Combine soy bean paste, sherry, salt and pepper in a small bowl, mix well and set aside. Blend cornstarch with a little water to a paste.
Heat oil in a wok or deep pan, when hot add prawns and cook until colored pink, lift out, drain and set aside.
Heat peanut oil in a wok or pan, add garlic and cook for 2 minutes, add onion and cook until transparent. Stir in sherry mixture and cook for 1 minute, add prawns and heat, add blended cornstarch and stir-fry for 1–2 minutes, until mixture thickens and is bubbling hot. Serve immediately with Fried Rice.

# Steamed Pork Rice Balls

Serves:  4–6
Cooking time:  30 minutes

　½ cup rice
　cold water
　4 dried mushrooms
　8 oz (230 g) can water chestnuts, drained
　3 scallions
　1 lb (500 g) lean pork
　1 teaspoon salt
　½ teaspoon glutamate
　½ teaspoon sugar
　2 slices root ginger, crushed
　1 egg, well beaten
　Plum Sauce — see recipe page 89

Soak rice overnight in a bowl of cold water, drain thoroughly and spread on a clean cloth to dry. Soak mushrooms in a bowl of hot water for 30 minutes, drain very well and mince. Chop water chestnuts and scallions very finely. Mince the pork and combine with salt, glutamate, sugar, ginger and egg in a bowl and mix well. Form mixture into small 1" (2½ cm) balls and roll carefully in the rice until well covered. Arrange balls in a large steamer, not touching, and steam over boiling water for 30 minutes. Make sure water does not touch steamer. Serve rice balls with Plum Sauce.
*(Illustrated on page 1.)*

▲ BEAN SPROUTS AND CRABMEAT SALAD (RECIPE PAGE 24)

▲ CHINESE RICE CAKE (RECIPE PAGE 24)

# Crab in Black Bean Sauce

Serves: 4–6
Cooking time: 10 minutes

*1½ lbs (2 × 375 g) cooked crabs*
*2 tablespoons black beans*
*1 tablespoon white vinegar*
*2 teaspoons cornstarch*
*2 tablespoons dry sherry*
*1 teaspoon salt*
*1 tablespoon sugar*
*⅓ cup chicken stock*
*4 scallions*
*3 tablespoons oil*
*2 cloves garlic, crushed*
*1 slice root ginger, crushed*
*parsley sprigs for garnish*

Wash crabs, lift off top shells and cut away the intestines. Rinse the inside of shell tops to clean. Remove claws and big nippers and crack them to scoop out meat. Chop down the center of each crab to halve, then chop each half into three equal portions, this will give 6 body sections from each crab.

Rinse black beans in a strainer under cold running water for a few seconds and drain, place in a small bowl with vinegar and mash beans well. Blend cornstarch with sherry and add to the mashed beans with salt, sugar and chicken stock and blend. Wash and chop scallions into 1″ (2½ cm) lengths.

Heat oil in a large wok or pan, add garlic and ginger and stir-fry for 1 minute, add crab portions and stir-fry for 2 minutes, add scallions and stir-fry a further 2 minutes. Pour black bean mixture over the crab and simmer for 5 minutes. Serve hot on a warm dish and decorate with crab shells, nippers, claws, and parsley.

# Bean Sprouts and Crabmeat Salad

Serves: 4
Cooking time: 2 minutes

16 oz (440 g) can crabmeat
1 oz (30 g) dry bean threads
½ lb bean sprouts
4 tablespoons white vinegar
2 teaspoons sesame oil
½ teaspoon salt
½ teaspoon glutamate
2 scallions

Drain crabmeat and break into bite size pieces. Soak bean threads in hot water until soft and transparent, drain well and cut into 4″ (10 cm) lengths. Pour bean sprouts into a pan, boil for 2 minutes and drain. Combine vinegar, sesame oil, salt and glutamate in a bowl, add the white part of scallions, cut into shreds and stir well. Add bean sprouts, bean threads and crabmeat and toss gently, cover with plastic film, chill for 1 hour and serve.
*(Illustrated on page 22.)*

# Chinese Rice Cake

Serves: 4–6
Cooking time: 50–55 minutes
Oven: 180°C 350°F

3 cups of hot cooked rice
¼ cup sugar
2 tablespoons butter
1 cup seeded, chopped dates
½ cup chopped, glacé cherries
¼ cup seeded, minced prunes
¼ cup minced raisins
¼ cup minced, preserved oranges
¼ cup minced, preserved ginger
extra 3 glacé cherries
extra 2 dates, seeded and halved
green angelic for decoration
2 tablespoons almond paste

**Syrup:**
⅓ cup sugar
1 cup (250 ml) water
1 teaspoon almond flavoring

To make syrup, combine sugar, water and almond flavoring in a pan and cook, stirring to dissolve sugar, for 1–2 minutes, then boil rapidly for 2 minutes. Pour into a small serving bowl and set aside to cool.
Stir sugar and butter through hot rice. Mix chopped dates and cherries in a bowl. Mix minced prunes, raisins, preserved oranges and ginger together in a separate bowl.
Grease an 7″ (18 cm) cake pan and add a 1″ (2½ cm) layer of rice, firm and spread dates and cherries in a layer. Add another layer of rice, followed by the minced fruit mixture, then firm the remaining rice on top. Place cake pan in a baking dish and add boiling water to reach halfway up the side of the pan. Cook in a moderate oven for 30 minutes, then turn out on a warm dish. Decorate with extra cherries and dates, angelic and almond paste and serve warm with almond syrup.
*(Illustrated on page 22.)*

# Marinated Pork

Serves: 4
Cooking time: 8–10 minutes

1 lb (500 g) lean pork
2 tablespoons soy sauce
4 tablespoons dry sherry
2 thin slices green ginger, crushed
1 teaspoon sugar
pinch salt
2 cloves garlic, crushed
2 tablespoons oil
2 teaspoons cornstarch
2 onions, sliced
2 green bell peppers, seeded and sliced
½ teaspoon glutamate
4 medium tomatoes, peeled and cut in wedges
Fried Rice — see recipe page 66

Cut pork into thin strips and place in a bowl, add soy sauce, sherry, ginger, sugar, salt and garlic, baste and set aside to marinate for 2 hours, basting occasionally.

Heat oil in a wok or pan until bubbling, lift pork from the marinade and add to the wok, stir-fry for 1–2 minutes, then lift out, drain and keep warm. Stir cornstarch into the marinade and mix.

Heat wok, add onions and bell peppers and stir-fry for 1–2 minutes. Return pork to the wok, add glutamate and stir, add the marinade and tomatoes and stir-fry for 1–2 minutes. Serve immediately with Fried Rice.

*(Illustrated on page 9.)*

# Deluxe Lemon Chicken

Serves:  4
Cooking time:  45–50 minutes

*3 lbs (1½ kg) chicken*
*salt*
*1 tablespoon light soy sauce*
*2 tablespoons sherry*
*1 teaspoon sugar*
*½ teaspoon glutamate*
*juice of 2 lemons*
*4 tablespoons oil*
*1 clove garlic, crushed*
*1 thin slice ginger root, crushed*
*1½ cups (375 ml) chicken stock*
*extra lemon, cut in rings*
*sprigs of parsley*
*Fried Rice — see recipe page 66*

Trim and rinse chicken, pat dry with paper towels and rub inside and out with salt. Mix soy sauce, sherry, sugar, glutamate and lemon juice in a bowl and stir well for a marinade. Brush chicken well with the marinade and set aside for 1 hour.

Heat oil in a large wok or pan, add garlic and ginger and stir gently for 1 minute, until oil is hot, then add chicken and cook for 5 minutes, turning to brown on all sides. Reduce heat, add stock, cover and simmer gently for 35–40 minutes, until tender.

Remove chicken from wok and cut into serving pieces, place on a warm dish and keep warm. Add the remaining marinade to the wok and heat quickly, then pour over the chicken pieces. Garnish with lemon rings and parsley sprigs and serve immediately with Fried Rice.

*(Illustrated on page 11.)*

# Mongolian Lamb with Bell Pepper

Serves:  4
Cooking time:  10–12 minutes

*1½ lbs (750 g) boned lamb shoulder*
*2 cloves garlic, crushed*
*2 slices fresh green ginger, crushed*
*grated rind and juice of 1 orange*
*1 tablespoon cornstarch*
*1 tablespoon soy sauce*
*½ cup peas, fresh or frozen*
*1 red bell pepper, seeded and finely chopped*
*1 teaspoon salt*
*1 tablespoon sherry*
*1 tablespoon water*
*2 tablespoons peanut oil*

Cut lamb into medium size strips and add to a bowl with garlic, ginger, orange rind, 1 teaspoon cornstarch, 1 teaspoon soy sauce, peas and bell pepper and mix, then set aside for 10 minutes. Meanwhile, blend the remaining cornstarch with salt, sherry, orange juice and water and mix well. Heat oil in a wok or pan over high heat, add the lamb mixture and stir-fry for 2 minutes, until meat browns slightly, then spoon back into the bowl. Add cornstarch mixture to the wok and stir-fry over heat for 2 minutes, until mixture thickens. Return lamb mixture to the wok and heat, stir for 2 minutes until boiling, reduce heat, cover and simmer for 2 minutes. Serve immediately.

*(Illustrated on page 7.)*

# Chicken Fillets with Baby Sweet Corn

Serves: 4
Cooking time: 10−12 minutes

2 whole chicken breasts
12 oz (350 g) can baby corn
1 carrot
1 teaspoon salt
1 teaspoon sugar
½ teaspoon glutamate
2 teaspoons light soy sauce
3 teaspoons cornstarch
1 tablespoon dry sherry
1 tablespoon peanut oil
1 slice fresh root ginger, crushed
½ cup (125 ml) chicken stock

Bone chicken breasts, discard skin and cut flesh into strips. Drain the corn; peel the carrot and cut into small strips. Combine salt, sugar, glutamate and soy sauce in a bowl, mix well and set aside. Blend cornstarch with sherry and set aside.

Heat oil in a wok or pan, add ginger and carrot and stir-fry for 2 minutes, add chicken strips and cook for 1 minute. Add the soy sauce mixture and stock and bring to the boil, reduce heat and simmer for 2−3 minutes. Increase heat, stir in blended cornstarch and stir-fry until thickened. Serve immediately.

CHOP SUEY (RECIPE PAGE 28) ▶

# Chop Suey

Serves: 4
Cooking time: 12–15 minutes

1 lb (500 g) lean pork
2 onions
1 green bell pepper
1 medium parsnip
1 cup (250 ml) strong meat stock
¼ teaspoon salt
¼ teaspoon sugar
1 tablespoon soy sauce
1 tablespoon dry sherry
4 oz bean sprouts
1 teaspoon cornstarch
Boiled Rice — see recipe page 86

Cut the pork into thin slices and cut onions into wedges. Seed bell pepper and cut into rings; peel parsnip and slice. Add pork slices and stock to a wok and cook until meat is tender, add onions, bell pepper and parsnip and stir-fry for 3 minutes. Stir in salt, sugar, soy sauce, sherry and bean sprouts and stir-fry for 3 minutes. Mix cornstarch with a little water and stir into the mixture, heat, stirring until thickened. Serve piping hot with Boiled Rice.
(Illustrated on page 27.)

# Banquet Lobster

Serves: 6–8
Cooking time: 4–6 minutes

4 lbs (2 kg) 2 cooked lobsters
4 scallions
1 tablespoon cornstarch
2 tablespoons water
3 tablespoons peanut oil
2 cloves garlic, crushed
2 thin slices root ginger, crushed
2 tablespoons dry sherry
1 tablespoon sugar
1 teaspoon salt
½ teaspoon sesame oil
½ cup (125 ml) chicken stock
parsley for garnish

Wash lobsters and drain. Place lobsters on their backs. Remove legs and nippers and chop off the heads. Clean out one head, wash and reserve for garnish. Using a cleaver, crack the shell of the nippers and remove the meat, chop down the length of lobsters and scoop out meat, but reserve one tail shell for garnish. Wash scallions and cut into 1" (2½ cm) lengths. Blend cornstarch with water to a smooth paste.
Heat oil in a wok or pan, add garlic, and ginger and stir-fry for 1 minute, add sherry, sugar, salt and sesame oil and stir-fry for 1 minute. Stir in scallions and lobster meat, add chicken stock and heat, stirring constantly, until boiling. Stir in cornstarch paste and cook for ½ a minute until mixture thickens. Spoon on to a warm platter, garnish with lobster head, tail, parsley, and serve.
(Illustrated on pages 2 & 3.)

# Stir-fried Shrimp and Vegetables

Serves: 4
Cooking time: 18–20 minutes

1 lb (500 g ) fresh shrimp
1 bunch broccoli
1 red bell pepper
4 scallions
2 stalks celery
1 tablespoon cornstarch
2 tablespoons water
4 tablespoons oil
1 clove garlic, crushed
3 thin slices ginger root, shredded
8 oz (230 g) can bamboo shoots, drained and sliced
10 oz (300 g) can baby corn, drained
1 teaspoon sugar
½ teaspoon salt
½ teaspoon glutamate
½ teaspoon sesame oil
1 tablespoon sherry
1 cup (250 ml) chicken stock

Leaving the tails on, shell and de-vein the shrimp. Cook the broccoli flowerettes in a pan of boiling, salted water for 7–8 minutes and drain, wash in cold water and drain again. Seed the bell pepper and cut into strips. Wash scallions and cut in 2″ (5 cm) lengths. Thinly slice celery, diagonally. Blend cornstarch with water in a bowl to a smooth paste. Heat 2 tablespoons of oil in a wok or pan, add garlic, ginger and scallions and stir-fry for 1 minutes, add shrimp and stir-fry for 1–2 minutes. Lift shrimp from the wok and set aside. Add remaining oil to the wok and heat, add broccoli, bamboo shoots, corn, celery and bell pepper and stir-fry for 1 minute, add sugar, salt, sesame oil, glutamate and sherry and stir-fry for 2 minutes. Return shrimp to the wok, add stock and bring quickly to the boil. Stir in cornstarch mixture and stir constantly until the mixture thickens. Serve immediately on warm plates.
*(Illustrated on page 5.)*

# Spring Rolls

Serves:  6–8
Cooking time:  20 minutes

*4 dried mushrooms*
*2 teaspoons cornstarch*
*1 tablespoon water*
*¼ Chinese cabbage, shredded*
*3 scallions, cut into 1″ (2½ cm) lengths*
*3 tablespoons oil*
*½ lb (250 g) lean pork*
*¼ lb (125 g) shelled shrimp*
*1 tablespoon soy sauce*
*1 teaspoon sugar*
*1 teaspoon salt*
*2 tablespoons chicken stock*
*10 Spring Roll Wrappers — see recipe page 86*
*oil for deep frying*

Soak mushrooms in water for 30 minutes, drain well and shred. Dissolve cornstarch in water. In a wok or pan sauté cabbage and scallions in 1 tablespoon of oil for 1 minute, lift out vegetables, drain and set aside.
Add remaining oil to the wok and heat, add pork, shrimp and mushrooms and stir-fry for 1 minute,

return cabbage and scallions to the wok and add soy sauce, sugar, salt and stock and stir-fry for 3–4 minutes. Add cornstarch mixture to thicken and remove from heat.
Divide the mixture into 10 portions and place each portion on the lower half of each wrapper. Roll wrappers over the filling, tucking in ends, into neat rolls, and seal with a flour paste. Deep fry rolls, five at a time, in hot oil for 4–5 minutes, until golden brown. Drain and serve hot.
*(Illustrated on page 15.)*

# Chinese Style Vegetables

Serves:  4–8
Cooking time:  18–20 minutes

*3 medium onions*
*3 medium carrots*
*½ medium cauliflower*
*½ medium cabbage*
*1 red bell pepper*
*1 green bell pepper*
*½ lb (250 g) zucchini*
*4 stalks celery*
*8 scallions*
*½ lb (250 g) green beans*
*¼ cup of peanut oil*
*2 slices of root ginger, chopped finely*
*1 cup of chicken stock*

Peel and quarter the onions, peel carrots and slice into thin rings. Wash cauliflower and cut into flowerettes, shred cabbage finely. Seed bell pepper and cut into rings and cut zucchini into thin slices. Cut celery diagonally into 1″ (2½ cm) pieces and chop scallions into 1″ (2½ cm) lengths. Top and trim beans and slice diagonally.
Heat oil in a wok or large pan, add ginger, onions, carrots and cauliflower and stir-fry to coat vegetables with oil. Add chicken stock and bring to the boil, cover and cook for 3 minutes. Add bell peppers, zucchini, celery, scallions and beans and stir-fry, cover and cook for 5 minutes. Remove lid, add cabbage and stir-fry, cover and cook a further 3 minutes, then serve.

# Prawn Salad

Serves: 4
Cooking time: 4 minutes

¾ lb (375 g) cooked prawns
2 slices ham
8 dried mushrooms
4 oz (125 g) bean sprouts
3 scallions
3 small carrots
4 tablespoons white vinegar
½ teaspoon salt
¼ teaspoon pepper
2 teaspoons sesame oil
¼ teaspoon glutamate

Shell and de-vein prawns. Cut ham into thin strips. Soak mushrooms in hot water for 20 minutes and drain well, discard stems and slice caps thinly. Pour bean sprouts into a pan, boil for 2 minutes and drain. Wash scallions and slice. Peel carrots, cut into small strips and boil in a little water for 2 minutes, drain and set aside.

In a small bowl, combine vinegar, salt, pepper, sesame oil and glutamate and stir well for the dressing. Combine mushrooms, bean sprouts, scallions, carrots and dressing in a salad bowl, add prawns and ham and toss lightly, chill and serve.

# Miniature Spring Rolls

Serves:   4–6
Cooking time:   15–18 minutes

½ lb (250 g) cooked shrimp, shelled
½ lb (250 g) ground pork
½ small bundle egg noodles
1 tablespoon butter
1 slice root ginger, crushed
2 dried mushrooms, soaked and chopped
3 scallions, finely chopped
1 teaspoon soy sauce
½ teaspoon salt
½ teaspoon glutamate
Wonton Wrappers — see recipe page 63
1 egg, beaten
oil for cooking
Sweet and Sour Sauce — see recipe page 90

Cook noodles in a pan of boiling water for 5 minutes, breaking noodles roughly. Heat butter in a pan, add pork and sauté until well browned, add ginger, mushrooms and scallions and cook for 1–2 minutes, then turn into a bowl. Add shrimp, noodles, soy sauce, salt and glutamate and mix well.
Place a heaped teaspoon of mixture down the center of each Wonton Wrapper and glaze edges with egg. Roll each wrapper over the filling, tuck in the ends and seal with egg. Deep fry in hot oil, until golden brown. Drain and serve immediately with Sweet and Sour Sauce.

# Vermicelli-Transparent Noodles

Serves:   allow 1 small bunch for each dish
Cooking time:   4–5 seconds per small bunch

300 g packet of vermicelli
oil for cooking

Cut the packet of vermicelli in half using a sharp knife, then separate each half into small bunches. Heat oil in a deep pan until very hot. Using tongs, carefully lower a small bunch of vermicelli into the oil, it will puff and become white, then rise to the surface in about 4–5 seconds, when it is cooked. Quickly lift out with a slotted spoon and drain on absorbent paper. Repeat the process with the remaining bunches.

# Almond Meat Balls

Serves:   6–8
Cooking time:   15–20 minutes

2 lbs (1 kg) lean beef
20 peeled almonds
1 tablespoon boiling water
¼ teaspoon saffron threads
2 medium onions
1 egg
1 tablespoon finely chopped parsley
2 teaspoons salt
2 slices ginger root, crushed
4 tablespoons cornmeal
3 tablespoons water
2 cups (500 ml) oil
Chinese chili sauce

Grind the beef finely. Soak almonds in a bowl with boiling water for 4 hours, then dry thoroughly. Pour 1 tablespoon boiling water over saffron threads in a small bowl and leave to soak. Peel onions and chop finely. Combine beef, egg, onions, parsley, salt, ginger and half the cornmeal in a dish and mix thoroughly, using the hands. Add soaked saffron threads with the liquid and mix well.

Divide mixture into 20 portions, place an almond in the middle of each portion and form into small balls. Place balls on a dish and chill for 1 hour. In a bowl, mix remaining cornmeal with 3 tablespoons of cold water for a very thin batter.
Heat the oil in a deep pan (or deep fryer to 175°C–340°F). Coat meat balls in the batter and lower into deep hot oil and cook, 4 at a time, for 3–4 minutes, until golden brown. Lift out the balls, drain on paper towels and keep hot. Serve piping hot with Chinese chili sauce.
*(Illustrated on opposite page.)*

# Pork and Cabbage Soup

Serves:   4–6
Cooking time:   1½–1¾ hours

8 cups (2 liters) water
2 lbs (1 kg) pork bones
1 teaspoon salt
3 peppercorns
1 teaspoon finely chopped coriander leaves
2 thin pieces root ginger, thinly sliced
1 clove garlic, crushed
½ lb (250 g) pork flank
3 cups Chinese cabbage
1 tablespoon cornstarch
2 tablespoons water
1 tablespoon sherry

Combine water, pork bones, salt, peppercorns, coriander, ginger and garlic in a large pan and bring to the boil, reduce heat, cover and simmer for 1¼–1½ hours. Remove from heat and let stand for 15 minutes, then strain stock into a separate pan. Discard rind from pork flank and slice meat into thin strips. Shred the cabbage finely. Blend cornstarch with water to make a thin paste. Bring stock to the boil, stir in blended cornstarch and boil for 3 minutes, add sherry, pork strips and cabbage. Return to the boil and cook for 4–5 minutes, until pork is tender. Stir well and serve piping hot.

ALMOND MEAT BALLS (RECIPE THIS PAGE) ▶

# Watermelon Fruit Salad

Serves: 6–8

½ watermelon, cut lengthways
1 cantaloupe
1 papaya
1 mango
18 oz (565 g) can lychees in heavy syrup
2 tablespoons dry sherry

Sponge the watermelon skin and dry, slice a little off the base of the melon to sit firmly. Using a melon baller, scoop out all the pink flesh into a bowl, discarding seeds, and chill the watermelon shell. Cut cantaloupe, papaya and mango in halves, discard seeds and membranes, scoop out balls of the flesh and add to the watermelon balls. Drain lychees, reserving the syrup, and add to the fruit.

Mix lychee syrup and sherry together, pour over the fruit and chill for at least 1 hour. Pour fruit and syrup into the watermelon shell and serve.

# Chili Prawns

Serves: 4
Cooking time: 8–10 minutes

1 lb (500 g) fresh prawns or shrimp
½ small Chinese cabbage
4 scallions
1 red bell pepper
1 large dried chili
1 tablespoon cornstarch
2 tablespoons water
2 tablespoons oil
1 clove of garlic, crushed
2 thin slices root ginger, crushed
½ teaspoon salt
1 teaspoon sugar
1 tablespoon soy sauce
2 tablespoons sherry
½ cup chicken stock
¼ cup unsalted peanuts

Shell and de-vein the prawns, rinse under cold water and drain. Wash cabbage and chop into pieces. Slice scallions into 1" (2½ cm) lengths. Wash and seed bell pepper and cut into thin rings. Split chili into 4 equal parts, lengthways, and discard seeds. Blend cornstarch with water in a bowl, to a thin paste and set aside.

Heat 1 tablespoon of oil in a wok or pan, add cabbage and stir-fry until coated with oil, remove from wok and keep hot. Add remaining oil to the wok and heat, add garlic, ginger and salt and stir-fry for 1 minute. Stir in bell pepper, chili, sugar, soy sauce and sherry and cook for 1 minute, add prawns and stir-fry for about 1 minute, until prawns turn pink. Add blended cornstarch and, stirring constantly, add stock, scallions and peanuts and cook for 1–2 minutes. Arrange cabbage on warm plates, spoon hot prawn mixture on top, and serve immediately.

# Chicken Balls with Lychees

Serves: 4–6
Cooking time: 12–15 minutes

1 lb (500 g) cooked chicken
½ lb (250 g) ham
1 medium onion
8 dried mushrooms
2 tablespoons cornstarch
1 teaspoon salt
2 tablespoons light soy sauce
1 tablespoon dry sherry
2 egg whites, stiffly beaten
flour
oil for deep cooking

**Sauce:**
2 tablespoons cornstarch
1 cup (250 ml) chicken stock
14 oz (425 g) can lychees in syrup
1 tablespoon dry sherry
1 tablespoon hoi sin sauce
2 scallions, finely chopped

For the sauce, blend cornstarch with a little stock to a smooth paste. Drain lychees, reserving ½ cup of the syrup. In a small pan, combine lychees and reserved syrup with remaining chicken stock, sherry and hoi sin sauce, bring to the boil and stir in blended cornstarch paste. Reduce heat, add scallions, heat and keep warm.

Bone and skin the chicken and chop finely. Chop ham finely. Peel and finely chop or mince onion. Soak mushrooms in hot water for 20 minutes, drain and pat dry, discard stems and chop caps finely. Combine cornstarch, salt, soy sauce and sherry in a bowl until smooth, add chicken and ham and mix — fold in beaten egg whites to blend. With floured hands, form the mixture into small balls.

Heat oil in a deep pan, or deep fryer, and cook the chicken balls, a few at a time, for 2−3 minutes, until golden brown. Lift out and drain on paper towels. Serve chicken balls and the hot sauce on warm plates immediately.

# Curried Chicken

Serves: 4
Cooking time: 10 minutes

*1 lb (500 g) cooked chicken*
*1 medium onion*
*1 stalk celery*
*2 teaspoons peanut oil*
*1 piece of root ginger, crushed*
*1−2 teaspoons curry powder, to taste*
*2 teaspoons cornstarch*
*1 cup (250 ml) chicken stock*
*¼ teaspoon glutamate*
*1 teaspoon soy sauce*
*¼ teaspoon salt*
*Boiled Rice — see recipe page 86*

Skin and bone the chicken and cut into serving pieces. Peel the onion and cut into thin wedges. Chop celery into small pieces.

Heat peanut oil in a wok or pan, add ginger and stir-fry for one moment, add onion and stir-fry for 1 minute, then add celery and stir-fry for 1 minute. Over low heat stir in curry powder and stir for 2 minutes. Blend cornstarch with chicken stock and stir into the wok with glutamate, soy sauce, salt and chicken pieces, and simmer for 5 minutes. Serve hot with Boiled Rice.

# Mushroom Soup

Serves: 4−6
Cooking time: 15−18 minutes

*¼ lb (125 g) fresh mushrooms*
*3 scallions*
*6 cups (1½ liters) chicken stock*
*1 slice root ginger, crushed*
*1 tablespoon sherry*
*½ teaspoon sesame oil*
*½ teaspoon glutamate*

Wash the mushrooms and chop into quarters. Cut the scallions into 1″ (2½ cm) lengths. Combine chicken stock and ginger in a large pan and bring to the boil, add mushrooms and scallions, reduce heat, cover and simmer for 10 minutes. Add sherry, sesame oil and glutamate and simmer for 2−3 minutes and serve.

# Deep Fried Scallops

Serves: 4
Cooking time: 6−8 minutes

*1 lb (500 g) scallops*
*cornstarch*
*1 egg*
*1 tablespoon milk*
*dry breadcrumbs*
*oil for deep frying*
*parsley, finely chopped*
*lemon wedges*
*Seafood Sauce — see recipe page 90*

Wash scallops, drain well and roll in cornstarch. Mix egg and milk together in a bowl and beat lightly, dip scallops in the egg mixture, then toss into the breadcrumbs to coat and chill for 1 hour. Dip again in egg mixture and toss in breadcrumbs a second time.

Heat oil in a deep pan, or in a deep fryer to 180°C (350°F), add scallops in two batches and cook each batch for 3−4 minutes, until golden brown. Drain on paper towels and serve hot, sprinkled with parsley and garnished with lemon wedges and Seafood Sauce.

▲ PORK AND BAMBOO SHOOTS (RECIPE PAGE 38)

▲ FISH FILLETS WITH VEGETABLES (RECIPE PAGE 38)

# Bean Sprout Salad

Serves:  4

8 oz (250 g) bean sprouts
8 oz (225 g) can baby corn
4 oz (105 g) can mussels
1 small carrot
¼ red bell pepper, seeded and thinly sliced
½ jar Chinese mixed pickles
2 tablespoons lemon juice

Carefully drain bean sprouts and set aside. Drain corn and mussels and cut each mussel in half. Peel carrot and slice into rings, seed bell pepper and slice finely. Combine corn and mussels in a bowl with mixed pickles, add carrot and bell pepper and mix. Sprinkle lemon juice over salad, toss and chill for 1 hour. Spread bean sprouts on top and serve.

# Fluffy Rice

Serves:  4–6
Cooking time:  40–45 minutes

1 cup long grain rice
1 teaspoon salt
2–2½ cups (500–625 ml) water

Place rice in a sieve and wash under running cold water to remove dust and excess starch, continue to wash until the water runs clear. Turn rice into a large pan with salt, add water to cover rice by 1″ (2½ cm) and bring to the boil, over high heat, and boil rapidly, stirring often to prevent sticking, until most of the water is absorbed. Reduce heat to low, cover tightly and allow rice to steam, undisturbed, for 20–30 minutes.

# Pork and Bamboo Shoots

Serves: 4
Cooking time: 6–7 minutes

   ¾ lb (375 g) lean pork
   1 tablespoon cornstarch
   2 tablespoons water
   1 medium onion, chopped
   1 clove garlic, crushed
   1 tablespoon white wine
   ½ teaspoon salt
   4 oz (125 g) can bamboo shoots
   1 tablespoon oil
   2 tablespoons oyster sauce
   1 teaspoon sugar
   Plum Sauce — see recipe page 89
   Hoi Sin Sauce

Slice pork into strips and then into 1″ (2½ cm) lengths and place in a bowl. Dissolve cornstarch in water. In a small bowl, combine onion, garlic, wine, salt and the dissolved cornstarch and mix well. Spoon over the pork and baste to coat meat well. Cut bamboo shoots into thin slices.
Heat oil in a wok or pan until hot, add meat mixture and stir-fry for 2 minutes, add bamboo shoots and stir-fry for 1 minute. Add oyster sauce and sugar and stir-fry for 1 minute. Serve immediately with the sauces.
*(Illustrated on page 36.)*

# Peking Dust

Serves: 4–6
Cooking time: 8–10 minutes

   14 oz (400 g) can unsweetened chestnut purée
   pinch of salt
   2 tablespoons sugar
   2 cups (500 ml) whipping cream
   1 tablespoon fine granulated sugar
   1 teaspoon vanilla extract
   8 oz (310 g) can mandarin oranges in light syrup
   1 tablespoon brown sugar
   4–5 glacé cherries

Combine chestnut purée, salt and sugar in a pan and heat, stirring to dissolve and blend sugar. Remove from heat and set aside until cold. In a bowl, whip the cream until slightly thickened, add fine granulated sugar and vanilla and beat until stiff. Divide cream in half and set one half aside to chill. Fold remaining cream into the chestnut mixture to blend, press gently into a greased mold and chill for 1 hour.
Meanwhile, drain mandarin oranges, place syrup in a pan with brown sugar, heat and stir, until sugar is dissolved, then cook rapidly for 2 minutes. Pour syrup into a bowl, cool and chill. Unmold chestnut mixture on to a dish, pour syrup over the top and decorate with cherries. Serve with mandarin oranges and remaining whipped cream.

# Fish Fillets with Vegetables

Serves: 4
Cooking time: 15–20 minutes

   1 lb (500 g) fish fillets
   2 tablespoons flour
   6 dried mushrooms
   1 bell pepper, seeded and sliced
   2 onions
   2 teaspoons cornstarch
   1 cup (250 ml) stock
   3 tablespoons peanut oil
   2 thin slices green ginger, crushed
   ½ teaspoon salt
   ½ teaspoon five spice powder
   1 tablespoon soy sauce
   Fluffy Rice — see recipe page 37

Cut fish into bite size pieces and dust with flour. Soak mushrooms in hot water for 30 minutes until soft, discard stems and cut caps into thin slices. Peel onions and cut into rings. Blend cornstarch and stock together and set aside.
Pour 2 tablespoons of oil in a wok or pan and heat until very hot, add a few pieces of fish at a time, and cook for 2–3 minutes, turning, until golden brown on all sides, lift out fish, drain on paper towels and keep hot. Add remaining oil and heat until hot, add

onions and stir-fry for 1 minute. Add mushrooms and bell pepper and stir-fry for 1 minute. Add ginger, salt and five spice powder and stir well. Stir in soy sauce and blended cornstarch and cook, stirring constantly, for 3 minutes. Serve vegetables and fish immediately with Fluffy Rice.
*(Illustrated on page 36.)*

# Stir-fried Mixed Vegetables

Serves:   4
Cooking time:   3 minutes

*8 oz bean sprouts*
*1 onion*
*1 red bell pepper*
*1 green bell pepper*
*2 stalks celery*
*1 cucumber*
*3 scallions*
*4 leaves of Chinese cabbage*
*2 tablespoons chicken stock*
*1 teaspoon salt*
*½ teaspoon glutamate*
*1 teaspoon sugar*
*2 teaspoons soy sauce*
*2 tablespoons oil*
*1 clove garlic, crushed*
*2 thin pieces of root ginger, crushed*
*2 teaspoons lemon juice*
*1 teaspoon sesame oil*

Drain the bean sprouts, peel onion and cut into thin wedges, remove seeds from bell peppers and cut into slices. Cut celery and scallions diagonally into 1″ (2½ cm) lengths. Peel and seed the cucumber and cut into small strips. Shred the cabbage leaves. In a small bowl, combine stock, salt, glutamate, sugar and soy sauce, mix well and set aside. Heat oil in a wok or pan, add garlic and ginger and stir-fry for a moment, add all the vegetables and the stock mixture, increase heat to high and stir-fry for 2 minutes, sprinkle with lemon juice and sesame oil, stir well and serve piping hot.

# Stuffed Crabs

Serves:   4
Cooking time:   4−5 minutes

*4 small blue swimmer crabs*
*½ lb (250 g) cooked prawns or shrimp*
*4 dried mushrooms*
*4 scallions*
*1 cup soft breadcrumbs, firmly packed*
*1 teaspoon salt*
*1 egg, beaten*

Carefully remove the top shell from each crab, wash shells thoroughly under running hot water and set aside. Remove the flesh from the body and claws of the crabs, chop finely and place in a bowl. Shell and de-vein prawns, mince finely and add to the crabmeat. Soak mushrooms in hot water for 20 minutes and drain, discard stems, chop caps finely and add to the crabmeat. Wash scallion, chop finely and add to the crabmeat with breadcrumbs, salt and beaten egg and mix thoroughly.
Divide mixture into four portions and spoon portions into cleaned crab shells. Place shells on a rack and grill for 4−5 minutes, until heated through and browned. Serve immediately.

# Pig's Knuckle Soup

Serves:   4
Cooking time:   2½−2¾ hours

*4 pig's knuckles*
*½ turnip*
*scallion tops*
*8 cups (2 liters) chicken stock*
*½ teaspoon salt*

Clean knuckles and chop into pieces. Peel and cut the turnip into 1″ (2½ cm) cubes. Slice the scallion tops. Place the knuckles in a large pan with chicken stock and salt and bring to the boil, skim off and impurities, reduce heat, cover and simmer for 2 hours. Add turnips and cook a further 30 minutes. Serve soup sprinkled with scallions.

▲

# Steamed Fish Chinese Style

Serves: 2
Cooking time: 15–18 minutes

3 lbs (1½ kg) whole carp or bream
salt
2 tablespoons light soy sauce
2 tablespoons sherry
2 tablespoons peanut oil
1 teaspoon sugar
1 piece of green ginger
2 scallions

Wash the fish and pat dry with paper towels, inside and out. Score both sides of the fish fleshy parts with a sharp knife and rub in salt. In a small bowl mix together soy sauce, sherry, peanut oil and sugar for a marinade. Peel ginger and cut into thin strips and slice scallions into 1" (2½ cm) lengths. Brush the fish on both sides with the marinade. Place in an ovenproof dish and strew with ginger and scallions. In a lidded pan, with a rack, or an electric frypan, pour water to a 1" (2½ cm) depth and heat to simmering, add the dish with fish, cover and steam for 15–18 minutes.
Meanwhile, slowly heat the remaining marinade in a pan and simmer for 1–2 minutes. Serve the fish with the hot marinade.

# Peking Soup

Serves: 4–6
Cooking time: 25–30 minutes

6 dried mushrooms
4 oz (125 g) can bamboo shoots
2 leeks
1 small Chinese turnip
6 cups (1½ liters) chicken stock
2 tablespoons tomato purée
2 teaspoons sesame oil
1 slice ginger root, crushed
salt and pepper

Soak mushrooms in hot water for 20 minutes, drain and discard stems, then cut caps into quarters. Drain bamboo shoots and slice. Wash the leeks and chop into 1" (2½ cm) lengths. Peel the turnip and cut into thin slices. Pour stock into a large pan, add bamboo shoots, mushrooms, leeks and turnip and bring to the boil, reduce heat slightly, cover and cook for 10 minutes. Add tomato purée, sesame oil, ginger, salt and pepper and stir, cover and simmer for 10–15 minutes, then serve.

▼

# Chinese Style Pork

Serves: 4
Cooking time: 10−12 minutes

1½ lbs (750 g) lean pork
8 oz (250 g) bean sprouts
4 spring onions
½ green bell pepper
4 tablespoons peanut oil
Boiled Rice — see recipe page 86

**Spice Sauce:**
1 tablespoon cornstarch
4 tablespoons white wine
⅓ cup soy sauce
¼ teaspoon salt
½ teaspoon sugar
1 slice root ginger, crushed

For the sauce, mix cornstarch with wine in a bowl to a smooth paste, stir in soy sauce, salt, sugar and ginger and mix well.
Cut pork into thin slices and marinade in the sauce for 20−25 minutes. Drain the bean sprouts, slice the spring onions, seed the bell pepper and cut into thin slices.
Lift pork slices from the marinade and drain. Heat peanut oil in a wok or pan, add pork and stir-fry for 4−5 minutes, remove and keep hot. Add onions, bean sprouts and bell pepper to the wok and stir-fry for 2−3 minutes. Return pork to wok, stir in marinade and cook, stirring until hot. Serve immediately with Boiled Rice.
(Illustrated on page 41.)

# Brussels Sprouts

Serves: 4
Cooking time: 12−15 minutes

1 lb (500 g) Brussels sprouts
1 stalk celery
1 onion
1 strip of bacon
salt
2 teaspoons peanut oil
1 clove garlic, crushed

Trim the Brussels sprouts and cut a cross in each base. Wash celery and finely chop. Peel onion and cut into rings. Discard rind and cut bacon into small squares. Add sprouts and salt to a pan of water and bring to the boil, reduce heat and simmer for 5 minutes, then drain.
Heat oil in a wok or pan, add garlic, onion and bacon and stir-fry for 1 minute. Add sprouts and celery and stir-fry for 2−3 minutes, then serve hot.

# Chocolate Ice Cream Balls

Serves: 10−12
Cooking time: 1−2 minutes

2 quart carton of full cream vanilla ice cream
2 tablespoons gelatin
4 tablespoons water
½ cup (125 ml) Tia Maria liqueur
½ lb (250 g) sweetened, dark cooking chocolate
¼ lb (125 g) lard
cocktail sticks

Place 2 oven trays and a small ice cream scoop in the freezer to chill. Allow ice cream to soften a little at room temperature, then spoon into a bowl. Soften gelatin in water in a small bowl, place bowl over a pan of simmering water and stir to dissolve, then cool, add to the ice cream with liqueur and beat until blended and smooth. Place bowl in the freezer for 8 hours or overnight, until hard frozen. Scoop small balls of ice cream and place on chilled trays. Insert a cocktail stick in each ball and return trays to the freezer, until balls are hard. Break chocolate into pieces and place, with lard, in a bowl over a pan of simmering water and stir until melted and blended, remove bowl from heat and cool. Working swiftly and using cocktail sticks to handle, dip ice cream balls into the chocolate, one at a time, to coat well. Replace balls on trays, carefully removing the sticks, and freeze until hard. Turn the balls into a container, cover and store in the freezer until required.
For a gala occasion, heap chocolate ice cream balls into a glass bowl, set the bowl in a larger glass bowl of crushed ice and serve at the table with coffee.

# Butterfly Prawns

Serves: 4
Cooking time: 8–10 minutes

1 lb (500 g) prawns
1 slice of lean rindless bacon
1 teaspoon soy sauce
½ teaspoon salt
1 tablespoon sherry
1 egg, beaten
dry breadcrumbs
oil for cooking
Chili Sauce — see recipe page 90

Retaining tails, shell and de-vein the prawns, cut a slit down the back of each prawn and press open. Cut bacon into 2″ (5 cm) thin strips. Mix soy sauce, salt and sherry in a bowl, add prawns and marinate for 1 hour. Lift out prawns and drain, press a bacon strip on the opened slit, carefully dip prawns into beaten egg and coat with breadcrumbs, pressing crumbs in well.

Heat oil in a wok or pan and cook prawns, a few at a time, for 2 minutes, until golden brown and crisp. Drain on paper towels and serve piping hot with Chili Sauce.

# Chicken and Walnuts

Serves: 4–6
Cooking time: 10–12 minutes

2 lbs (1 kg) chicken breasts
1 teaspoon salt
2 teaspoons sugar
3 tablespoons sherry
1 tablespoon light soy sauce
3 tablespoons cornstarch
1 tablespoon extra cornstarch
¾ cup (185 ml) chicken stock
4 tablespoons oil
1 cup chopped walnuts
2 cloves garlic, crushed
1 thin slice root ginger, crushed
1 egg, beaten
1 teaspoon glutamate

Bone the chicken breasts and cut into 1″ (2½ cm) pieces. Combine salt, 1 teaspoon of sugar, sherry and soy sauce in a bowl, add chicken and baste, then set aside to marinate for 20 minutes. With a slotted spoon, lift chicken from the marinade and drain, but reserve the marinade. Dust chicken well with cornstarch. Blend extra cornstarch with stock. Heat oil in a wok or pan, until bubbling, add walnuts and sauté 1 minute, lift out walnuts, drain and set aside. Add garlic and ginger to the wok and stir-fry for 1 minute. Dip chicken pieces into beaten egg, then add to the wok and cook for 2–3 minutes, stirring occasionally. Add glutamate, remaining sugar and reserved marinade and stir well, reduce heat, cover and simmer for 3 minutes. Remove lid, add cornstarch stock and bring to the boil, stirring constantly, until the mixture thickens. Add walnuts, stir through and serve immediately on warm plates.

# Fish Soup

Serves: 4–6
Cooking time: 25–30 minutes

1½ lbs (750 g) fish fillets, (cod, etc.)
⅔ cup of rice
½ teaspoon salt
6 cups (1½ liters) chicken stock
2 eggs
2 teaspoons peanut oil
1 tablespoon sherry
1 piece root ginger, crushed
2 scallions, finely chopped

Clean and bone the fish, then flake. Wash the rice and drain, then place in a large pan with half the flaked fish, salt and stock and bring to the boil. Reduce heat, cover and simmer until rice softens and liquid is thick. In a bowl, combine eggs with remaining fish, peanut oil, sherry and ginger and mix well, then stir into the soup and simmer for 1–2 minutes. Serve soup piping hot, sprinkled with scallions.

▲ ORIENTAL SPRING ROLLS (RECIPE PAGE 46)

▲ GLAZED DUCK WITH LEEKS (RECIPE PAGE 46)

# Sweet and Sour Fish

Serves:   2–4
Cooking time:   8–10 minutes

1 large whole bream or small snapper
1 cup flour
½ teaspoon salt
¼ teaspoon pepper
2 teaspoons cornstarch
½ cup (125 ml) water
4 scallions
1 medium carrot
1 thin slice of root ginger, finely minced
4 tablespoons oil
2 tablespoons sugar
⅓ cup vinegar
1 tablespoon sherry
2 teaspoons light soy sauce
1 tablespoon tomato catsup
½ cup Chinese mixed pickles

Wash fish in salted water and pat dry, remove eyes and trim fins and tail. Score three or four times across the back with a sharp knife and coat lightly with flour, seasoned with salt and pepper. Blend cornstarch with water in a bowl to a smooth paste. Chop scallions into 1″ (2½ cm) lengths. Peel carrot and cut into small strips.

Cook ginger lightly in a small pan with 2 teaspoons of oil, add sugar, vinegar, sherry, soy sauce, tomato sauce, carrot, scallions and pickles. Stir over medium heat for 1 minute, stir in cornstarch paste and bring to the boil, stirring constantly, until the sauce thickens, about 2 minutes, and keep hot. Heat the remaining oil in a wok or pan over medium heat, add the fish and cook for 2 minutes, until lightly browned, turn and brown other side for 2 minutes. Lift out carefully on to a hot serving plate, pour the sauce over and serve immediately.

# Glazed Duck with Leeks

Serves: 4–6
Cooking time: 1½ hours
Oven: 200°C reduce to 180°C
400°F reduce to 350°F

3 lbs (1½ kg) dressed duck
2 tablespoons dry sherry
1 tablespoon soy sauce
¼ teaspoon five spice powder
dash of pepper
1 tablespoon honey
5 leeks
pinch of salt
½ cup (125 ml) water

Wash duck well and pat dry, remove neck and giblets. Combine sherry, soy sauce, five spice powder, pepper and honey in a small pan and heat gently until honey is melted and marinade is smoothly blended. Simmer for 2 minutes, remove from heat and cool.
Brush marinade over inside and outside of duck; reserve remaining marinade for the sauce. Wrap duck in foil, place in an ovenproof dish and cook in a hot oven for 20 minutes. Reduce heat to moderate and cook a further 60 minutes.
Meanwhile, wash and chop leeks and place in an ovenproof casserole dish with salt and water. Cover and cook in a moderate oven for 30 minutes. Remove duck from foil and place on a serving dish, serve in slices with strained leeks and warmed marinade as a sauce.
(Illustrated on page 44.)

# Crispy Lemon Fish

Serves: 4–6
Cooking time: 4–5 minutes

2 lbs (1 kg) fish fillets
flour
salt and pepper
3 cups (750 ml) oil for cooking
Lemon Sauce — see recipe page 90
chopped parsley

**Batter:**
6 tablespoons self-raising flour
¼ teaspoon baking powder
½ teaspoon salt
1 egg, lightly beaten
3 tablespoons water
1 tablespoon lemon juice

For the batter; sift flour, baking powder and salt into a bowl, add egg and mix, gradually stir in water and lemon juice and mix to a smooth batter. Skin and bone the fish and cut into approximately 2″ (5 cm) pieces. Coat the fish pieces in flour, seasoned with salt and pepper, then dip into the batter to cover well. Lift out with a slotted spoon and cook in a deep pan (or deep fryer at 180°C — 350°F) of hot oil for 4–5 minutes, until golden brown. Lift out and drain on paper towels. Serve fish on warm plates, pour hot Lemon Sauce on top and sprinkle with parsley.

# Oriental Spring Rolls

Serves: 6–8
Cooking time: 30–35 minutes

1 cup of finely chopped chicken
2 teaspoons soy sauce
2 thin slices green ginger, crushed
1 teaspoon dry sherry
4 dried mushrooms
3 teaspoons cornstarch
1 tablespoon water
3 tablespoons oil
4 thinly chopped
½ lb (250 g) shelled prawns or shrimp
1 tablespoon extra soy sauce
1 teaspoon sugar
12 Spring Roll Wrappers — see recipe page 86
little beaten egg white
2 cups (500 ml) peanut oil for deep frying
Seafood Sauce — see recipe page 90

Mix chicken with soy sauce, ginger and sherry in a bowl and allow to marinate for 10 minutes. Soak mushrooms in hot water until soft, drain, discard stems and slice caps thinly. Blend cornstarch with water in a small bowl.

Heat 1 tablespoon of oil in a wok or pan and stir-fry chicken mixture for 1 minute, until browned, then remove from the wok. Heat remaining oil in the wok, add mushrooms and scallions and stir-fry for 1 minute. Add prawns, chicken mixture, extra soy sauce, sugar and blended cornstarch and stir until mixture boils and thickens, about 1 minute, then allow to cool. Divide mixture and spoon on to the lower half of each wrapper, fold lower edge over and tuck in sides, roll into neat rolls and seal with a little egg white.

Heat peanut oil in a wok, or electric fry pan 150°C (300°F) add spring rolls, 4 at a time, and cook for 8–10 minutes, turning to brown on all sides. Drain on paper towels, then serve hot with the sauce. *(Illustrated on page 44.)*

# Chicken with Asparagus

Serves:  4
Cooking time:  10–12 minutes

*¾ lb (375 g) chicken pieces*
*1 stalk celery*
*1 red bell pepper*
*4 scallions*
*8 oz (250 g) can whole baby corn*
*8 oz (250 g) can asparagus tips*
*1 egg white*
*2 tablespoons cornstarch*
*6 tablespoons peanut oil*
*1 tablespoon sherry*
*oil for cooking*
*1 slice of fresh root ginger, crushed*
*1 tablespoon light soy sauce*
*2 tablespoons chicken stock*

Bone and skin the chicken pieces and cut into small pieces. Slice celery diagonally, into pieces. Cut bell pepper in half remove seeds, slice thinly and slice scallions. Drain the corn and asparagus. In a bowl, beat egg white, stir in 1 tablespoon of cornstarch and 2 tablespoons peanut oil and beat until smooth, add chicken and stir to coat well. Blend remaining cornstarch with sherry in a bowl and set aside.
Heat the oil in a wok or pan and when hot, add chicken pieces and cook for 2–3 minutes, until light golden. Lift out chicken and drain on paper towels. Pour off oil.

Heat remaining peanut oil in a wok or pan, add ginger, scallions and bell pepper and stir-fry for 1 minute, add chicken, soy sauce, baby corn, chicken stock and sherry blended cornstarch. Stir until the mixture thickens and boils. Add asparagus, stir lightly and simmer for 2–3 minutes. Serve immediately on warm plates.

# Braised Prawns and Vegetables

Serves:  4–6
Cooking time:  10–12 minutes

*1½ lbs (750 g) fresh prawns or shrimp*
*8 dried mushrooms*
*4 scallions*
*½ lb (250 g) broccoli*
*1 cup (250 ml) salted water*
*1 tablespoon cornstarch*
*3 tablespoons water*
*¾ cup (185 ml) chicken stock*
*1 tablespoon sherry*
*1 teaspoon hoi sin sauce*
*3 tablespoons peanut oil*
*1 clove garlic, crushed*
*2 pieces syruped ginger, finely cut*
*½ teaspoon salt*
*1 teaspoon sugar*
*Crisp Fried Noodles — see recipe page 81*

Shell and de-vein prawns and cut in half lengthways. Soak mushrooms in hot water for 20 minutes and drain, discard stems and cut caps into strips. Wash scallions and cut into 1″ (2½ cm) lengths. Wash broccoli and cut into thick pieces, boil in a pan with salted water for 2 minutes and drain well. Blend cornstarch with water in a small bowl. Combine stock, sherry and hoi sin sauce in a bowl and mix.
Heat peanut oil in a wok or pan, stir in garlic, ginger and scallions and stir-fry for 1 minute, add prawns and stir-fry for 2 minutes. Remove prawns and scallions, drain and set aside. Re-heat oil, stir in mushrooms and broccoli and stir, add salt, sugar and stock mixture and stir well. Cover and cook for 2 minutes, Remove lid, return prawns and scallions, stir in cornstarch mixture and bring to the boil, stirring to thicken. Serve immediately over crisp noodles.

# Chicken and Broccoli

Serves: 4
Cooking time: 10–12 minutes

2 whole chicken breasts
½ bunch of broccoli
1 teaspoon salt
1 teaspoon sugar
2 teaspoons light soy sauce
2 teaspoons sherry
1 teaspoon cornstarch
2 teaspoons chicken stock
1 tablespoon peanut oil
1 slice fresh root ginger, crushed
Crisp Fried Noodles — see recipe page 81

Bone and chicken breasts, discard the skin and cut meat into strips. Wash the broccoli and break into small stalks. Combine salt, sugar, soy sauce and sherry in a bowl, mix well and set aside for the sauce. Blend cornstarch with chicken stock in a small bowl and set aside.
Heat peanut oil in a wok or pan, add ginger and stir-fry for 1 minute, add the chicken and stir-fry for 1 minute. Add the sauce mixture and broccoli and bring to the boil, stirring, reduce heat, cover and simmer for 3–4 minutes, remove lid, increase heat, add cornstarch stock and stir-fry until mixture thickens. Place noodles on warm plates, spoon chicken and broccoli on top and serve hot.

# Pork and Mushrooms

Serves: 4
Cooking time: 6–7 minutes

½ lb (250 g) lean pork
2 slices ham
8 dried mushrooms
4 oz (125 g) bamboo shoots
4 scallions
1 tablespoon cornstarch
1 cup (250 ml) chicken stock
3 tablespoons oil
1 slice ginger root, crushed
½ teaspoon salt
pinch of pepper
¼ teaspoon glutamate
1 tablespoon soy sauce
Boiled Rice — see recipe page 86

Cut pork into bite size pieces and slice ham into thin strips. Soak mushrooms in hot water for 20 minutes and drain, pat dry and chop roughly. Drain bamboo shoots and cut into thin slices. Wash scallions and cut into 1″ (2½ cm) lengths. Blend cornstarch with chicken stock.
Heat oil in a wok or pan, add pork and ham and stir-fry for 2 minutes, lift out and set aside. Heat oil to hot, add ginger, scallions and mushrooms and stir-fry for 1 minute. Return pork and ham to wok, add salt, pepper and glutamate, then stir in cornstarch blended stock and stir-fry for 2 minutes. Stir in soy sauce, reduce heat, cover and simmer for 1–2 minutes. Serve with Boiled Rice.

▼

# Beef Steak with Spinach

Serves: 4
Cooking time: 12–15 minutes

*1 lb (500 g) beef steak*
*2 tablespoons sherry*
*1 tablespoon soy sauce*
*1 teaspoon sugar*
*¼ teaspoon glutamate*
*½ teaspoon sesame oil*
*1 bunch of spinach*
*½ teaspoon cornstarch*
*2 tablespoons beef stock*
*4 tablespoons peanut oil*
*1 piece of root ginger, crushed*

Remove all fat and sinew from meat and cut into ¼" (5 mm) strips, then cut in half and gently pound with a meat mallet. Marinate meat in a bowl with sherry, soy sauce, sugar, glutamate and sesame oil for 1 hour. Wash spinach, cut out stalks and slice leaves into pieces. Cut two of the spinach stalks, diagonally, into 1" (2½ cm) lengths. Blend cornstarch with the stock.
Heat 2 tablespoons of oil in a wok, add ginger and spinach stalks and stir-fry for 3 minutes, lift out and drain. Add remaining oil to the wok and heat until hot, add meat, a few pieces at a time, and stir-fry for 2 minutes, until meat changes color, lift out and drain. When all meat is lightly cooked, return it to the wok with ginger and spinach stalks and stir-fry until boiling. Add spinach, marinade and stock and stir-fry, over high heat, for 3–4 minutes.

# Pomegranate Cocktail

Serves: 4–6

*6 pomegranates*
*½ cup sugar*
*1 cup (250 ml) water*
*3 cups (750 ml bottle) of champagne*

Allow the pomegranates to rest in a warm place for five days or until the skin is a light brown color.

Rub the fruit on a hard surface back and forth several times, until fruit opens up. Cut in half and squeeze out the juice into a pan, add sugar and water and heat, stirring until the sugar is dissolved, then remove from heat and cool. Stir in half the bottle of champagne and mix, pour liquid into ice cube trays and freeze until set. Place frozen cubes in chilled glasses, top with remaining champagne and serve.

# Pork Chow Mein

Serves: 6
Cooking time: 8–10 minutes

*1 lb (500 g) lean pork*
*8 dried mushrooms*
*2 tablespoons cornstarch*
*1 cup (250 ml) chicken stock*
*2 tablespoons soy sauce*
*salt*
*4 scallions*
*2 stalks celery*
*4 tablespoons peanut oil*
*2 medium onions, very thinly sliced*
*1 red bell pepper, seeded and sliced*
*4 oz (125 g) bean sprouts*
*Crisp Fried Noodles — see recipe page 81*

Cut pork into 1" (2½ cm) slices. Soak mushrooms in hot water for 30 minutes and drain, discard stems and cut caps into thin slices. In a bowl, mix cornstarch with a little stock to a smooth paste, gradually stir in remaining stock, soy sauce and salt, until mixture is fairly salty. Cut scallions into 1" (2½ cm) pieces and diagonally slice the celery, finely.
Heat two tablespoons of oil in a wok or large pan over high heat. When oil is hot, add pork slices and stir-fry for 1–2 minutes, until brown, then lift meat from the wok and set aside. Add the remaining oil and heat, add onions and celery and stiry-fry for 1 minute. Add mushrooms, bell pepper, scallions and bean sprouts and cook for 1 minute, stirring. Stir in cornstarch mixture and heat, stirring, for 1–2 minutes, until mixture thickens. Return pork to the wok and stir for 2 minutes, until meat is hot and sauce is clear. Serve immediately over Crisp Fried Noodles.
*(Illustrated on page 49.)*

# Savoury Prawn Fritter

Serves: 4
Cooking time: 14–16 minutes

*1 lb (500 g) fresh prawns or shrimp*
*1 egg*
*¾ cup flour*
*1 cup (250 ml) milk*
*½ teaspoon salt*
*3 scallions, finely chopped*
*oil for deep cooking*
*Vermicelli — Transparent Noodles — see recipe*
*   page 32*

Shell and de-vein prawns, rinse and pat dry, then mince finely. Combine egg, flour and milk in a bowl and mix thoroughly to a smooth batter, add salt, prawns and scallions and blend.
Heat oil in a deep fryer or deep pan until hot, add large tablespoons of the mixture, one at a time, and cook for 3–4 minutes, until golden brown. Lift out, drain on paper towels and keep hot. When all fritters are cooked, serve on a bed of Transparent Noodles with a dipping sauce.

# Sautéed Mixed Vegetables

Serves: 4–6
Cooking time: 10–12 minutes

*1½ lbs (750 g) sliced vegetables*
*½ cup (125 ml) chicken stock*
*1 tablespoon oyster sauce*
*1 teaspoon soy sauce*
*½ teaspoon salt*
*½ teaspoon glutamate*
*2 teaspoons cornstarch*
*1 tablespoon water*
*2 tablespoons peanut oil*
*1 clove garlic, crushed*
*1 piece of root ginger, crushed.*

Use a mixture of Chinese cabbage, leeks, cauliflower, scallions, brussels sprouts, broccoli, peas, beans, zucchini or celery, in any combination. In a bowl, combine stock, oyster and soy sauces, salt and glutamate and mix well for the sauce. Blend cornstarch with water to a smooth paste.
Heat oil in a wok or pan with garlic and ginger until hot, add the vegetables and stir-fry for 2 minutes. Add sauce mixture and cover, reduce heat and simmer for 4–5 minutes. Push vegetables to one side of the wok, add blended cornstarch and stir until the sauce thickens, stir vegetables through the thickened sauce and serve immediately.

# Chinese Omelette

Serves: 2
Cooking time: 8–10 minutes

*¼ lb (125 g) selected meat or fish*
*3 dried mushrooms*
*2 scallions*
*3 eggs*
*¾ cup (185 ml) milk*
*pinch of glutamate*
*2 teaspoons lard or oil*

**Sauce:**
*1 teaspoon cornstarch*
*½ cup (125 ml) water*
*2 teaspoons oyster sauce*
*1 teaspoon soy sauce*

For the sauce, blend cornstarch with water in a pan, stir in oyster and soy sauces and bring to the boil, stirring until thickened, reduce heat and gently simmer for 1 minute, then keep warm.
This recipe calls for ¼ lb (125 g) of either prawns, shrimp, lobster, crab, chicken, pork, 12 oysters or mixed bacon and peas.
Soak mushrooms in hot water for 20 minutes, drain and pat dry, discard stems and chop caps finely. Wash and finely chop scallions. Beat eggs well in a bowl and stir in milk and glutamate until blended. Heat lard or oil in a wok or pan, add selected meat or fish with mushrooms and scallions and lightly stir-fry for 1 minute. Stir the wok contents into the beaten egg mixture and mix well.
Re-heat wok, add the egg mixture and cook the omelette, until barely set and lightly browned on the under side, fold omelette over and cook a further 1 minute. Place omelette on a warm plate, add sauce on top and serve.

▲ SWEET AND SOUR PORK (RECIPE PAGE 54)

▲ CHICKEN AND ALMONDS (RECIPE PAGE 55)

# Crab and Corn Soup

Serves: 4–6
Cooking time: 12–15 minutes

 8 oz (200 g) can crabmeat, drained
 8 oz (230 g) can creamed corn
 6 cups (1½ liter) chicken stock
 3 teaspoons cornstarch
 1 tablespoon dry sherry
 1 egg
 salt to taste

In a large pan, combine crabmeat, creamed corn and chicken stock and bring to the boil. Blend cornstarch with sherry and add to the pan. Beat egg, then slowly stir into the soup, simmer for 4–5 minutes, salt to taste and serve.

# Egg Flower Soup

Serves: 4
Cooking time: 8–10 minutes

 6 cups (1½ liters) chicken stock
 4 tablespoons sherry
 ½ teaspoon glutamate
 salt and pepper to taste
 1½ teaspoons sesame oil
 2 eggs
 2 scallions

Bring stock to the boil in a large pan, add sherry, glutamate, salt, pepper and sesame oil, cover and simmer for 3–4 minutes. Beat the eggs well and pour slowly into the soup, stir once or twice, then serve with chopped scallions.

# Combination Soup

Serves: 4
Cooking time: 20–25 minutes

    ¼ lb (125 g) chicken meat
    ¼ lb (125 g) pork
    ¼ lb (125 g) ham
    ¼ lb (125 g) fresh shrimp
    ¼ lb (125 g) scallops
    4 dried mushrooms
    4 scallions
    ½ Chinese cabbage
    2 teaspoons salt
    1 tablespoon sherry
    ½ lb (250 g) egg noodles
    6 cups (1½ liters) chicken stock

Dice the chicken, pork and ham into 1″ (2½ cm) pieces. Shell the shrimp and cut scallops in half. Soak mushrooms in hot water for 20 minutes and drain, discard stems and slice the caps. Wash the scallions and chop into 2″ (5 cm) lengths. Wash the cabbage and shred finely.
Combine chicken, pork, ham, mushrooms, scallions, cabbage, salt, sherry, noodles and stock in a large pan and bring to the boil, stirring to separate the noodles. Reduce heat, cover and simmer for 10 minutes. Add shrimp and scallops and simmer a further 5 minutes.

# Eggs in Pork Gravy

Serves: 4
Cooking time: 50–55 minutes

    4 eggs
    ½ lb (250 g) pork flank
    4 tablespoons soy sauce
    2 tablespoons sherry
    ½ teaspoon salt
    ½ teaspoon sugar
    ½ cup (125 ml) water

Boil the eggs in a pan of water for 7–8 minutes, cool and shell. Cut pork into 1″ (2½ cm) cubes and place in a pan with soy sauce, sherry, salt, sugar and water and bring to the boil. Reduce heat and simmer for 15 minutes, add eggs and baste with the gravy. Simmer for 30 minutes, until eggs are dark colored and liquid is reduced by half, then serve hot.

# Sweet and Sour Pork

Serves: 4
Cooking time: 12–15 minutes

    1 lb (500 g) lean pork
    1 green bell pepper
    2 canned pineapple rings
    4 scallions
    ⅓ cup sugar
    ½ cup (125 ml) vinegar
    2 teaspoons soy sauce
    3 tablespoons tomato catsup
    ½ cup (125 ml) water
    2 thin slices of green ginger, crushed
    2 tablespoons cornstarch
    2 tablespoons dry sherry
    1 egg
    extra cornstarch
    oil for deep cooking
    1 tablespoon peanut oil

Pound the pork with a mallet and cut into bite size pieces. Seed bell pepper and cut into small chunks, cut pineapple rings into wedges and cut scallions into 1″ (2½ cm) lengths.
Combine sugar, vinegar, soy and tomato sauces, water and ginger in a bowl. Mix well and set aside for the sauce mixture. Blend cornstarch with sherry in a small bowl and set aside. Lightly beat egg in a bowl, add pork pieces and stir to cover well. Lift out pork, a piece at a time and roll in extra cornstarch. Heat oil in a wok or deep pan until hot, add pork and cook over medium heat for 3–4 minutes, until golden brown. Lift out and drain on paper towels and keep warm.
Heat peanut oil in a wok or pan until hot, add bell pepper and scallions and stir-fry for 2 minutes. Add sauce mixture and bring to the boil, add pineapple and blended cornstarch and stir until the mixture thickens. Place pork on warm plates, spoon vegetables and sauce on top and serve piping hot.
*(Illustrated on page 52.)*

# Chicken and Corn Soup

Serves: 4–6
Cooking time: 10–12 minutes

½ lb (250 g) cooked chicken meat
6 cups (1 ½ liters) chicken stock
4 oz (100 g) can creamed corn
4 oz (100 g) can corn niblets
½ teaspoon salt
1 teaspoon sesame oil
1 tablespoon cornstarch
1 tablespoon dry sherry
1 egg
2 tablespoons of chopped scallions

Finely shred the chicken meat. In a large pan combine stock, creamed corn and niblets, salt and sesame oil and bring to the boil. Blend cornstarch with the dry sherry and add to the soup. Beat the egg and slowly pour into the soup, stirring, add chicken to the soup, simmer for 4–5 minutes and serve, topped with scallions.

# Chicken and Almonds

Serves: 4
Cooking time: 18–20 minutes

1 ½ lbs (750 g) chicken pieces
1 tablespoon cornstarch
1 tablespoon dry sherry
1 egg white, lightly beaten
1 teaspoon salt
1 teaspoon sesame oil
8 oz (250 g) can bamboo shoots
1 ¼ cups shelled almonds
1 tablespoon butter
oil for deep frying
2 tablespoons peanut oil
1 thin slice root ginger, crushed
½ cup green peas, fresh or frozen

**Sauce:**
1 tablespoon cornstarch
1 tablespoon sherry
2 teaspoons soy sauce
2 teaspoons oyster sauce
1 cup (250 ml) chicken stock

For the sauce, mix cornstarch with sherry in a bowl until smooth, add the remaining ingredients and stir until blended.

Bone the chicken pieces, discard the skin and slice flesh into 1″ (2½ cm) pieces. Blend cornstarch with sherry in a bowl, add egg white, salt and sesame oil and mix until smooth, add chicken and stir. Drain bamboo shoots and cut into wedges. Cook almonds in a pan with butter for 2–3 minutes.

Heat oil in a wok or deep pan, lift chicken pieces from the batter and lower into hot oil, a piece at a time, and cook for 2–3 minutes, but do not brown, drain well on paper towels and keep warm.

In a separate wok or pan, heat peanut oil, add ginger and bamboo shoots and stir-fry for 1 minute, add peas and the sauce mixture and bring to the boil, stirring, until the mixture thickens. Reduce heat, add chicken and simmer, stirring, for 1 minute. Serve immediately, sprinkled with almonds.
*(Illustrated on page 52.)*

# Sweet and Sour Tuna

Serves: 4
Cooking time: 5–7 minutes

14 oz (425 g) can of chunky tuna
1 large onion
2 bell peppers, 1 red, 1 green
2 canned pineapple rings
1 tablespoon peanut oil
Sweet and Sour Sauce — see recipe page 90
2 tablespoons Chinese mixed pickles
Boiled Noodles — see recipe page 86
Boiled Rice — see recipe page 86

Drain the tuna and break into small pieces. Peel the onion and cut into wedges, seed bell peppers and cut into chunks. Cut pineapple rings into wedges.

Heat oil in a wok or pan, add onion and Bell peppers and stir-fry for 1 minute, until onion is transparent, add pineapple and stir-fry for 1 minute. Stir in the sweet and sour sauce with Chinese pickles and stir-fry for 1 minute. Add the tuna and cook for 2 minutes, gently stirring. Serve on warm plates with Boiled Noodles or Boiled Rice.

# Oriental Curried Beef

Serves: 4
Cooking time: 25–30 minutes

1 lb (500 g) round steak
2 onions
1 turnip
½ lb (250 g) tomatoes
2 teaspoons cornstarch
1 tablespoon sherry
2 tablespoons oil or lard
½ teaspoon salt
½ teaspoon glutamate
2 teaspoons mild curry paste
1 teaspoon five spice powder
2 whole cloves
1 cup (250 ml) beef stock

Trim meat of fat and sinew and cut into 1″ (2½ cm) cubes. Peel onions and chop finely. Peel turnip and cut into small chunks. Peel tomatoes and chop roughly. Blend cornstarch with sherry in a small bowl.

Heat 1 tablespoon of oil or lard in a wok or deep pan. When hot, add meat and sauté for 1–2 minutes, remove to a dish and sprinkle with salt and glutamate. Add remaining oil to the wok, and heat, add onions and stir-fry for 1 minute. Stir in curry paste and cook for 1 minute, add tomatoes and cook, stirring constantly, for 2 minutes. Add five spice powder and cloves and stir in the stock. Return meat to the wok and add turnip, cover tightly and simmer for 15 minutes. Remove lid, stir in cornstarch mixture and cook, stirring, for 2–3 minutes. Serve hot.

PRAWN BALLS (RECIPE PAGE 58) ▶

# Prawn Balls

Serves: 4
Cooking time: 10–12 minutes

 ½ lb (250 g) shelled prawns or shrimp
 ⅔ cup dry, soft breadcrumbs, firmly packed
 2 tablespoons chicken stock
 1 teaspoon salt
 2 thin slices ginger root, crushed
 2 water chestnuts, crushed
 1 egg, separated
 3 cups (750 ml) peanut oil
 Lemon Sauce — see recipe page 90

Finely chop or mince the prawns. Combine bread crumbs, stock, salt, ginger, water chestnuts and egg yolk in a bowl and mix well. Beat egg white until stiff, then fold into the mixture, add prawns and mix well.
Heat oil in a wok or deep fryer to 180°C (350°F). Scoop walnut size portions of the mixture and form into balls, lower balls into hot oil and cook, 6 balls at a time, for 2–3 minutes, until golden brown. Remove balls with a skimming ladle and drain on paper towels. Serve hot with Lemon Sauce.
(Illustrated on page 57.)

# Gingered Steak

Serves: 4
Cooking time: 6–8 minutes

 1 lb (500 g) whole fillet steak
 1½ teaspoons cornstarch
 2 teaspoons soy sauce
 2 teaspoons sesame oil
 3 thin slices root ginger
 1 teaspoon sugar
 ½ teaspoon salt
 2 tablespoons dry white wine
 2 tablespoons peanut oil
 3 scallions finely chopped

Trim fat from meat and freeze for 30 minutes, then cut into ¼″ (5 mm) slices. Blend cornstarch with soy sauce in a bowl, until smooth, then stir in sesame oil and mix well, add the meat slices, baste and marinate for 30–35 minutes, basting occasionally, until absorbed. Slice ginger into fine strips and place in a bowl with sugar, salt and wine and mix well.
Heat peanut oil in a wok or pan, add meat a few slices at a time in one layer, and cook quickly on each side, lift out and keep warm. Add ginger mixture to the wok and stir-fry for 1 minute. Return meat to the wok and stir-fry for 1 minute. Serve immediately on warm plates, sprinkled with scallions.

# Combination Chicken and Vegetables

Serves: 4
Cooking time: 10–12 minutes

 1½ lbs (750 g) chicken pieces
 2 stalks celery
 8 dried mushrooms
 1 onion
 1 carrot
 6 scallions
 1 tablespoon cornstarch
 1 tablespoon sherry
 1 egg white, lightly beaten
 1 teaspoon salt
 1 teaspoon sesame oil
 2 tablespoons peanut oil
 1 piece of root ginger, crushed
 Boiled or Fluffy Rice — see recipes
    pages 86 & 37

**Sauce:**
 1 tablespoon cornstarch
 2 teaspoons soy sauce
 2 teaspoons oyster sauce
 1 tablespoon sherry
 1 cup (250 ml) chicken stock

For the sauce, mix cornstarch with soy and oyster sauces and sherry, until smooth, gradually stir in chicken stock until blended, and set aside.
Bone and skin the chicken pieces and cut meat into bite size pieces. Wash celery and cut, diagonally, into 1″ (2½ cm) pieces. Soak mushrooms in hot water for 20 minutes and drain, discard stems and cut caps into small pieces. Peel onion and cut into wedges, scrape the carrot and cut into rings and

chop the scallions into 1" (2½ cm) lengths. Blend cornstarch with sherry in a bowl, add beaten egg white, salt and sesame oil and mix well, add chicken, stir to coat well and set aside to marinate for 10 minutes, then lift out chicken.

Heat peanut oil in a wok or pan, add chicken and stir-fry for 1–2 minutes, until light golden, lift out and drain on paper towels and keep warm. Reheat the wok, add ginger, onion and carrot and stir-fry for 1 minute, add celery, mushrooms and scallions and stir-fry for 1 minute. Stir in remaining marinade and the sauce mixture, bring to the boil and stir-fry, until mixture thickens. Reduce heat, add chicken and simmer for 2 minutes. Serve on warm plates with Boiled or Fluffy Rice.

# Stir-fried Beef and Mushrooms

Serves:　4–6
Cooking time:　10–12 minutes

　*1 lb (500 g) rump or topside beef*
　*8 dried mushrooms*
　*4 scallions*
　*14 oz (425 g) can baby corn*
　*½ lb (250 g) French cut green beans*
　*1 medium carrot*
　*1 tablespoon cornstarch*
　*3 tablespoons water*
　*boiling salted water*
　*4 tablespoons oil*
　*1 teaspoon salt*
　*1 teaspoon sugar*
　*½ teaspoon glutamate*
　*1 tablespoon soy sauce*
　*2 tablespoons sherry*
　*½ cup (125 ml) beef stock*

Trim meat and cut across the grain into thin strips, 2" (5 cm) long. Soak mushrooms in hot water for 20 minutes and drain, discard stems and slice caps into thin strips. Wash scallions and cut into 2" (5 cm) lengths. Drain corn. Top and trim beans and slice, diagonally, into 2" (5 cm) pieces. Peel the carrot and slice into thin rings. Blend cornstarch with water to a thin paste. Par-boil carrot and beans

in boiling, salted water for 2 minutes, then drain. Heat 2 tablespoons of oil in a wok or pan, over medium to high heat, add half the meat and stir-fry for 1 minute, until browned, then lift out. Add remaining meat and stir-fry for 1 minute and re-move. Reduce heat to medium, add remaining oil and heat. Add beans, carrot, mushrooms and scallions and stir-fry for 2 minutes. Add baby corn, salt, sugar and glutamate and stir-fry for 1 minute. Stir in soy sauce, sherry and stock and thicken with blended cornstarch. Stirring constantly, return meat to the wok and cook for 2 minutes. Serve immediately on warm plates.

# Beef and Bell Peppers

Serves:　4
Cooking time:　8–10 minutes

　*1 lb (500 g) rump or top round steak*
　*2 thin slices root ginger, very finely chopped*
　*1 clove garlic, crushed*
　*1 tablespoon soy sauce*
　*2 medium onions*
　*1 medium red bell pepper*
　*1 medium green bell pepper*
　*2 teaspoons cornstarch*
　*1 tablespoon water*
　*2 tablespoons oil*
　*1 teaspoon sugar*
　*¼ teaspoon five spice powder*
　*1 tablespoon dry sherry*
　*½ cup (125 ml) stock*
　*Fried Rice — see recipe page 66*

Trim fat from meat and discard, cut steak into short thin strips and place in a bowl with ginger, garlic and soy sauce, stir well and set aside to marinate for 30 minutes, stirring occasionally. Peel onions and cut into thin wedges. Wash bell peppers, seed and cut into thin strips. Blend cornstarch with water to a thin paste.

Heat oil in a wok or pan over fairly high heat, add meat and marinade with onions and cook, stirring, for 2–3 minutes, until brown. Reduce heat to medium, stir in sugar, five spice powder, sherry and bell peppers and stir-fry for 2–3 minutes. Stir in stock and blended cornstarch and cook, stirring, for 2–3 minutes, until mixture thickens. Serve immediately on warm plates with Fried Rice.

## Combination Beef and Chicken

Serves: 4–6
Cooking time: 10–12 minutes

½ lb (250 g) rump steak
½ lb (250 g) cooked chicken breasts
8 dried mushrooms
2 stalks celery
1 medium onion
2 pieces preserved ginger
2 teaspoons cornstarch
1 tablespoon water
2 tablespoons peanut oil
¼ teaspoon glutamate
½ teaspoon salt
¼ cup chicken stock
1 teaspoon sugar
1 tablespoon soy sauce
1 tablespoon dry sherry
Boiled Rice — see recipe page 86

Slice beef into thin strips. Bone chicken and break into pieces. Soak mushrooms in hot water for 20 minutes and drain, discard stems and halve the caps. Wash and slice celery into 1″ (2½ cm) lengths, peel onion and cut into rings, slice ginger into pieces and blend cornstarch with water into a paste.

Heat 1 tablespoon of oil in a wok or pan, add meats and stir-fry for 1–2 minutes. Remove meat and drain on paper towels. Add remaining oil to the wok and heat, add onion and stir-fry for 1–2 minutes. Add celery and ginger and stir-fry for 1–2 minutes. Add mushrooms, glutamate, salt, stock, meat and chicken and stir-fry for 1 minute. Stir in sugar, soy sauce, cherry and blended cornstarch and stir-fry until mixture thickens. Serve immediately with Boiled Rice.

## Traditional Peacock Platter

This dish derives its name from the various cold meats arranged on a platter to resemble the beautiful span of a peacocks tail. There is no precise recipe. It can be as extravagent or as simple as money and imagination will allow. All the meats used are cooked, then sliced thinly when cold. Sucking pig is the center piece, surrounded by ham, abalone, roast pork, shrimp, asparagus and fried duck, garnished with cooked transparent onions and broccoli, as seen in the photograph. Sliced hard boiled eggs, radish roses, cucumber slices, carrot flowers, pineapple wedges and other things can be used for decoration. Hoi Sin Sauce, Soy Sauce and Plum Sauce are served as dips. Recipes pages 89 & 91.

GINGER DUCKLING (RECIPE PAGE 62) ▶

# Ginger Duckling

Serves:  4–6
Cooking time:   12 minutes

*4 lbs (2 kg) dressed duckling*
*1 whole leek*
*2 scallions*
*1 small carrot*
*1½ tablespoons peanut oil*
*1 tablespoon thinly sliced preserved ginger*
*2 teaspoons ginger syrup*
*½ teaspoon freshly ground black pepper*
*2 tablespoons soy sauce*
*1 teaspoon salt*
*6 tablespoons chicken stock*
*Boiled Rice — see recipe page 86*

Wash and dry the duck, cut in half, remove bones and cut meat and skin into thin slices. Wash leek and scallions and cut into 1" (2½ cm) lengths. Peel the carrot and cut into very thin small slices about 2" (5 cm) long.

Heat 1 tablespoon oil in a wok or pan, add duck slices and stir-fry for 5 minutes, then remove and drain. Add remaining oil to the wok and heat, add ginger, scallions and carrot and stir-fry for 1 minute, stir in ginger syrup, black pepper, soy sauce, salt and chicken stock and stir-fry for 1 minute. Return duck to the wok, reduce heat and cook for 5 minutes, stirring occasionally. Serve immediately with Boiled Rice.

*(Illustrated on page 61.)*

# Sweet Potato Balls

Serves:  4
Cooking time:   10–12 minutes

*1 lb (500 g) sweet potatoes*
*salted water*
*1 egg*
*3 tablespoons sugar*
*1 tablespoon flour*
*3 tablespoons water*
*sesame seeds*
*oil for cooking*

Peel sweet potatoes, cut into pieces and place in a pan with salted water, bring to the boil and cook for 4–5 minutes, until soft, then strain and sieve to a purée, into a bowl, and cool. Beat egg and sugar, in a bowl, and add to the purée and mix thoroughly, then form into small balls. Mix flour and water to a thin paste, dip balls to coat and roll in sesame seeds. Lower into a pan of hot oil, a few at a time, and cook for 2–3 minutes, until golden brown. Lift out sweet potato balls, drain on paper towels and serve.

# Satay Beef

Serves:  4
Cooking time:   8–10 minutes

*1 lb (500 g) lean beef*
*1 tablespoon soy sauce*
*1 piece of green ginger, crushed*
*1 clove garlic, crushed*
*½ teaspoon sugar*
*½ teaspoon salt*
*1 teaspoon sesame oil*
*2 medium onions*
*3 tablespoons oil*

**Sauce:**
*1 teaspoon cornstarch*
*3 tablespoons beef stock*
*1 tablespoon satay sauce*
*1 teaspoon oyster sauce*
*1 tablespoon sherry*
*dash of Tabasco sauce*

Combine sauce ingredients in a bowl, mix well and set aside.

Freeze meat for 30 minutes to firm, then cut into ¼" (5 mm) slices and pound lightly to flatten. Combine soy sauce, ginger, garlic, sugar, salt and sesame oil in a bowl and mix well. Add meat slices, baste and set aside to marinate for 30 minutes. Peel onions and cut into wedges.

Heat oil in a wok or pan, add the meat slices and stir-fry for 1–2 minutes, until browned on each side, then lift from the wok and keep warm. Add onions to the wok and stir-fry until transparent. Stir in sauce mixture and any remaining marinade and bring to the boil, stirring, return the meat and stir-fry for 1 minute. Serve immediately on warm plates.

# Whole Chicken Soup

Serves: 4–6
Cooking time: 1½–1¾ hours

2 lbs (1 kg) chicken
6 cups (1½ liters) water
½ cup of rice
1 stalk celery
1 onion
2 teaspoons salt
½ teaspoon five spice powder
1 clove garlic, crushed
1 piece of green ginger, crushed

Place chicken in a large pan with the water. Wash the rice and add to the chicken. Cut celery into 1" (2½ cm) pieces, peel the onion and cut into small wedges. Add celery, onion, salt, five spice powder, garlic and ginger to the chicken and bring to the boil. Skim well, reduce heat, cover and simmer for 1½ hours. Lift out chicken and cool slightly, then cut into serving pieces and keep warm. Serve the soup first, followed by the chicken pieces with a dipping sauce.

# Fried Squid

Serves: 4
Cooking time: 6–8 minutes

1 lb (500 g) baby squid
boiling salted water
3 tablespoons flour
salt and pepper to taste
1 tablespoon peanut oil
1 tablespoon light soy sauce
1 tablespoon oyster sauce
Boiled Rice — see recipe page 86
lemon wedges

Prepare the squid and cut into 3" (7½ cm) pieces, slash the inner side in a criss cross pattern and cook in a pan of boiling salted water for 2 minutes. Drain and pat dry with paper towels and roll in flour, seasoned with salt and pepper.
Heat peanut oil in a wok or pan and when hot, add soy and oyster sauces and stir, add the squid and cook for 3 minutes, stirring constantly. Lift out and serve on warm plates with Boiled Rice and lemon wedges.

# Wonton Wrappers

Makes 40–50 wrappers

2 cups flour
1 teaspoon salt
1 egg
water
cornstarch

Sift flour and salt together into a bowl, make a well in the center and add the egg and 2 tablespoons of water, mix well, gradually add more water until a pliable dough, then knead until smooth.
Lightly dust a board with cornstarch, divide dough into two pieces and roll out each piece, until paper thin. With a sharp knife, cut into 3" (7½ cm) precise squares for Dim Sims, or 2½" (6 cm) precise squares for Wontons, or use a 3" (7½ cm) cutter for Gow Gees. Cover with a damp cloth until ready for use.
Wrappers, dusted with cornstarch, stacked and sealed in plastic film or bag, can be frozen.

# Steamed Chicken

Serves: 4–6
Cooking time: 40–45 minutes

2 lbs (1 kg) chicken
2 scallions, cut into 1" (2½ cm) lengths
1 slice fresh root ginger, crushed
salt
2 tablespoons white wine

Wash the chicken and pat dry with paper towels. Rub salt well into the skin, place scallions and ginger in the cavity and close with skewers. Place chicken on a rack and sprinkle with wine, place rack in a pan over 1" (2½ cm) of simmering water, cover tightly and steam for 40–45 minutes. Remove chicken and cool slightly, dissect into serving pieces and serve on warm plates with a dipping sauce.

# Beef Steak Canton Style

Serves:   4
Cooking time:   12–15 minutes

1 lb (500 g) beef steak
1½ teaspoons cornstarch
2 teaspoons soy sauce
1 egg yolk
¼ teaspoon baking soda
2 teaspoons peanut oil
⅓ cup water
1 tablespoon oil
1 thin slice root ginger, crushed
Fried Rice — see recipe page 66

## Sauce:
2 teaspoons soy sauce
2 teaspoons barbecue sauce
¼ teaspoon salt
¼ teaspoon sugar
1 tablespoon water

Combine all ingredients for the sauce in a small bowl and mix well.

Cut the steak, across the grain, into ¼" (5 mm) slices, then flatten slices with a meat mallet. Combine cornstarch, soy sauce, egg yolk, soda, peanut oil and water in a bowl and mix until smooth, add steak slices and marinate for at least 1 hour, basting occasionally.

Heat oil in a wok or pan with crushed ginger. When hot, add steaks, a few at a time, and stir-fry for 2 minutes each side, until all meat has been cooked, add sauce and stir-fry for 1 minute. Spoon steaks and sauce onto warm plates, garnish with tomato slices and serve hot with Fried Rice.

# Abalone Soup

Serves: 4
Cooking time: 12–15 minutes

*7 oz (200 g) can abalone*
*3 oz (100 g) bamboo shoots*
*4 dried mushrooms*
*4 scallions*
*4 cups (1 liter) chicken stock)*
*1 teaspoon soy sauce*
*1 teaspoon salt*

Drain the liquid from the abalone into a bowl and reserve; slice abalone very thinly. Drain bamboo shoots and cut thinly. Soak mushrooms in hot water for 20 minutes and drain, discard stems and slice the caps. Cut scallions into 1" (2½ cm) lengths.
Bring stock to the boil in a large pan and add mushrooms, bamboo shoots and scallions. Reduce heat and simmer for 5 minutes, add abalone and reserved liquid, soy sauce and salt, simmer for 2–3 minutes, and serve.

# Seafood Platter

Serves: 6
Cooking time: 15–18 minutes

*12 fresh prawns or 24 shrimp*
*12 oysters*
*12 scallops*
*2 baby squid*
*2 fish fillets*
*1 egg, beaten*
*dry breadcrumbs*
*flour*
*oil for deep cooking*
*parsley sprigs*
*lemon wedges*
*Sweet and Sour Sauce — see recipe page 90*

**Batter:**
*4 tablespoons self-raising flour*
*½ teaspoon salt*
*½ teaspoon baking soda*
*1 egg, beaten*
*4 tablespoons water*

For the batter, sift flour, salt and soda into a bowl, make a well and add the egg, gradually stir in water until a smooth batter. Cover with a cloth and set aside.
Retaining tails, shell and de-vein the prawns, slice the backs, open up and flatten. Dry oysters and scallops with paper towels. Clean the squid and cut into 6 pieces, slash the inner side in a diamond pattern and dry well. Bone the fish and cut into 1" × 2" (2½ cm × 5 cm) pieces. Dip prawns, oysters and scallops in beaten egg and roll in breadcrumbs, place on a dish, cover with plastic wrap and chill. Coat fish and squid with flour and dip in the batter.
Heat oil in a deep pan until hot, add fish and squid and cook for 4–5 minutes, until golden brown, lift out, drain on paper towels and keep warm. Add prawns, oysters and scallops to the hot oil and cook until light golden brown, then drain on paper towels.
Serve the seafood on a warm platter, garnished with parsley sprigs and lemon wedges, with Sweet and Sour Sauce.

# Chicken with Bell Peppers

Serves: 4
Cooking time: 6–8 minutes

*1 lb (500 g) boned chicken meat*
*2 red bell peppers*
*1 green bell pepper*
*2 tablespoons peanut oil*
*1 teaspoon salt*
*1 slice of fresh root ginger, crushed*
*½ teaspoon sugar*
*2 teaspoons light soy sauce*
*1 teaspoon cornstarch*
*2 teaspoons dry sherry*

Cut chicken meat into bite size pieces. Seed the bell peppers and slice into rings. Heat 1 tablespoon of oil in a wok or pan, when hot add the bell peppers and salt and stir-fry for 1 minute, lift out and drain on paper towels.
Add remaining oil to the wok and heat, add ginger and chicken and stir-fry for 1 minute, then stir in sugar and soy sauce. Blend cornstarch with sherry and stir into the wok and stir-fry, until slightly thickened. Return the bell peppers, cook 1–2 minutes and serve hot.

# Peking Chicken

Serves: 4
Cooking time: 6–8 minutes

*1 lb (500 g) cooked chicken*
*6 dried mushrooms*
*2 green bell peppers*
*2 onions*
*3 teaspoons cornstarch*
*1½ tablespoons water*
*3 tablespoons peanut oil*
*salt and pepper*
*3 tablespoons light soy sauce*
*1 tablespoon sherry*
*1 teaspoon sugar*
*3 tablespoons chicken stock*
*Soya-Sherry Dip — see recipe page 91*

Bone the chicken and break into pieces. Soak mushrooms in hot water for 20 minutes, drain and pat dry, discard stems and cut caps into quarters. Seed bell peppers and slice. Peel onions and cut into thin wedges. Blend cornstarch with water.
Heat 1 tablespoon of oil in a wok or pan until hot, add the onions and stir-fry for 1 minute, add bell peppers and stir-fry for 1 minute, remove both and drain on paper towels. Add remaining oil and heat, add mushrooms, chicken, salt and pepper and stir-fry for 1 minute, add soy sauce, sherry, sugar and stock and stir-fry for 1 minute. Return onions and bell peppers to wok, stir in blended cornstard and cook until slightly thickened. Serve immediately with the dipping sauce.

▼

# Oriental Fried Rice

Serves: 6–8
Cooking time: 6–8 minutes

*4 cups cooked rice*
*½ lb (125 g) bacon*
*3 scallions*
*3 canned pineapple rings*
*3 tablespoons oil*
*1 egg, beaten with a pinch of salt*
*½ lb (125 g) shelled prawns or shrimp*
*½ teaspoon salt*
*½ teaspoon glutamate*
*2 teaspoons soy sauce*

Allow cooked, drained rice to stand over night to dry and separate. Discard rind and cut bacon into ½″ (1 cm) squares. Wash scallions and cut into small lengths; cut pineapple rings into small wedges. Heat 1 tablespoon of oil in a wok or pan, pour in beaten egg and cook, without stirring. Lift out egg and cut into small squares and set aside. Heat remaining oil in the wok, and bacon, scallions and prawns and stir-fry, and rice and cook for 2 minutes, stirring and tossing constantly, to heat evenly. Season with salt and glutamate, add pineapple and egg squares and stir-fry for 1 minute. Sprinkle with soy sauce and serve hot.

BAKED PARCHMENT CHICKEN (RECIPE PAGE 68) ▶

# Baked Parchment Chicken

Serves: 4
Cooking time: 50 minutes
Oven: 180°C 350°F

1½ lbs (750 g) fresh chicken
1 whole leek
1 stalk of celery
4 tablespoons peanut oil
½ cup green peas
2 thick slices green ginger, crushed
1 tablespoon light soy sauce
2 teaspoons glutamate
1 teaspoon sugar
8 oz (230 g) can water chestnuts, drained
4 large squares parchment paper
Boiled or Fluffy Rice — see
   recipes pages 86 & 37

Wash the chicken and cut in half, then bone and cut flesh into bite size pieces. Wash the leek, pat dry and cut in ½" (1 cm) lengths, chop celery. Heat oil in a wok or pan, over high heat. Add chicken and stir-fry for 3–4 minutes. Add celery, leek, peas and ginger and stir-fry for 1 minute. Add soy sauce, glutamate and sugar and stir-fry for 1 minute. Lastly add water chestnuts and stir-fry for 1 minute. Divide mixture into 4 portions and place each portion on a parchment square, fold over the mixture to make into neat rolls and seal. Place rolls on a greased oven tray and cook in a pre-heated moderate oven for 40 minutes. Serve in the parchment with Boiled or Fluffy Rice.
(Illustrated on page 67.)

# Soft Fried Noodles

Serves: Allow 1 bundle per person
Cooking time: 1–2 minutes per bundle

16 oz (454 g) packet (10 bundles) fine noodles
4 tablespoons peanut oil

Soak noodles in a bowl of hot water for 8–10 minutes, separating the strands, then drain and spread on a tray lined with absorbent paper for 30 minutes to dry. Sprinkle with a little oil to prevent sticking.
Heat the remaining oil in a wok until very hot and starts to bubble. Add 1 bundle of noodles at a time and stir-fry with a spatula, making sure noodles do not mash. Cook for 1–2 minutes until translucent and light golden, then lift out and serve.
Or, add soaked, drained and dried noodles to the flavored oil or gravy in a wok, after vegetables or meat have been cooked, and cook until heated through, then lift out and serve.

# Seafood Combination

Serves: 6
Cooking time: 10–12 minutes

½ lb (250 g) squid
1 lb (500 g) fresh prawns or shrimp
½ lb (250 g) fish fillets
3 stalks celery
4 oz (125 g) bamboo shoots
1 small carrot
flour
salt and pepper
1 teaspoon cornstarch
1 tablespoon sherry
1 egg white, beaten
½ teaspoon grated ginger
boiling salted water
6 tablespoons oil
1 tablespoon peanut oil

**Sauce:**
2 teaspoons cornstarch
½ cup (125 ml) chicken stock
1 tablespoon sherry
1 tablespoon light soy sauce

For the sauce, blend cornstarch with stock in a bowl, stir in sherry and soy sauce until smooth, then set aside.
Cut squid into 1" (2½ cm) pieces and slash the edges. Shell the prawns, bone the fish and cut into 1" (2½ cm) pieces. Cut celery into 1" (2½ cm) diagonal slices, drain the bamboo shoots and cut into thin slices, peel the carrot and cut into thin rings. Roll squid in flour, seasoned with salt and pepper. In a bowl, blend cornstarch with sherry,

egg white and ginger and mix well, then add prawns and fish and stir. Par-boil carrots and bamboo shoots in a pan of boiling salted water for 2 minutes, add the celery and cook for half a minute and drain immediately.

Heat oil in a wok or deep pan, add prawns and fish and cook for 1 minute, add squid and cook for 2 minutes, then remove and drain on paper towels. In a separate wok or pan heat peanut oil, add vegetables and stir-fry for 2 minutes, add seafood and stir in sauce mixture. Cook, stirring, for 1–2 minutes, until mixture is slightly thickened, then serve immediately on warm plates.

# Scrambled Eggs and Crabmeat

Serves:  4
Cooking time:  4–5 minutes

*4 eggs*
*2 scallions, finely chopped*
*salt and pepper*
*1 tablespoon peanut oil*
*7 oz (200 g) can crabmeat, drained*

Beat the eggs in a bowl, add scallions, salt and pepper. Heat the peanut oil in a wok or pan, add the crabmeat and cook gently for 1 minute. Increase heat and when hot, stir in the egg mixture and cook, stirring, for 3 minutes, until eggs begin to set, but are still moist. Lift out and serve.

# Chilled Rice Pudding

Serves:  8–10
Cooking time:  20–25 minutes

*4 cups (1 liter) water*
*1 teaspoon salt*
*2 cups rice*
*½ lb (250 g) dates, seeded*
*20 red glacé cherries*
*¼ cup sugar*
*2 tablespoons mixed fruit peel*
*1 cup shredded coconut*
*⅔ cup (165 ml) cream, lightly whipped*

In a pan, bring water and salt to the boil and add rice, reduce heat slightly and cook for 20 minutes. Drain rice well and set aside to cool for 30 minutes. Chop dates into small pieces and chop 10 of the cherries.

Combine rice, dates, cherries, sugar, mixed peel and coconut in a bowl and mix well, then fold in cream. Turn into a greased mold, press firmly, cover with foil or plastic wrap and chill overnight. Unmold onto a dish, decorate with remaining cherries and serve.

# Satay Prawns

Serves:  4–6
Cooking time:  6–8 minutes

*1½ lbs (750 g) fresh prawns*
*1 teaspoon sugar*
*1 teaspoon cornstarch*
*¼ teaspoon of salt*
*pinch of glutamate*
*pinch of five spice powder*
*1 teaspoon soy sauce*
*1 teaspoon oyster sauce*
*1 tablespoon sherry*
*3 tablespoons satay sauce*
*2 onions*
*3 tablespoons peanut oil*
*water*

Shell and de-vein prawns, rinse and pat dry. Combine sugar, cornstarch, salt, glutamate and five spice powder in a bowl, stir in soy and oyster sauces and mix until smooth, gradually stir in sherry and satay sauce. Add prawns and baste well, then set aside to marinate for at least 1 hour. Peel onions and cut into wedges.

Heat peanut oil in a wok or large pan, add onions and stir-fry for 2 minutes, until transparent. Stir in prawns and marinade, with 3–4 teaspoons of water. Heat and stir-fry for 3–4 minutes, until prawns are pink and mixture is piping hot, then serve.

▲ BARBECUED PORK (RECIPE PAGE 72)

▲ DEEP FRIED HONEY KING PRAWNS (RECIPE PAGE 72)

# Deluxe Fried Rice

Serves:  4
Cooking time:  10–12 minutes

1 strip of bacon
1 lb (500 g) prawns or shrimp
4 dried mushrooms
4 scallions
1 tablespoon peanut oil
1 egg
salt and pepper to taste
3 cups boiled rice, drained and cooled
½ cup fresh or frozen peas
2 teaspoons soy sauce

Remove rind and cut bacon into ½″ (1 cm) squares. Shell the prawns and chop into small pieces. Soak mushrooms in hot water for 20 minutes, discard stems and cut caps into ½″ (1 cm) slices. Wash and chop scallions into ¼″ (5 mm) lengths.

Brush the inside of the wok or pan with a little oil, add bacon and stir-fry for 1 minute, lift out, drain and set aside. Add the remaining oil to the wok and heat, add egg, salt and pepper to taste and stir-fry to scramble. Add 1 cup of rice and stir-fry until egg combines with the rice, then add the remaining rice, the mushrooms and peas and stir-fry for 1 minute. Add bacon, prawns and scallions and stir-fry for 1 minute. Sprinkle with soy sauce, stir-fry until well blended and serve.

# Barbecued Pork

Serves: 4–6
Cooking time: 45–50 minutes
Oven: 230°C reduce to 200°C
450°F reduce to 400°F

1½ lbs (750 g) pork flank
3 cloves garlic, crushed
1 slice root ginger, crushed
2 teaspoon sugar
1 teaspoon salt
¼ teaspoon five spice powder
1 tablespoon soy sauce
1 tablespoon sherry
1 tablespoon honey
Chinese plum sauce
hoi sin sauce

Using a sharp knife, remove rind from the pork, or have the butcher do this. Combine garlic, ginger, sugar, salt, five spice powder, soy sauce, sherry and honey in a large dish and mix well, add pork, baste well and set aside to marinate for at least 1 hour, basting often.
Line a baking dish with foil and place a wire rack on top. Remove pork from the marinade and place on the rack, brush with marinade and cook in a very hot oven for 25–30 minutes, brushing with the marinade every 10–12 minutes. Turn pork over, brush with the pan drippings, reduce heat to hot and cook a further 15–20 minutes, until well glazed and caramelized with honey marinade. Cut meat into 1" (2½ cm) slices and serve with both sauces.
(Illustrated on page 70.)

# Pork Balls

Serves: 4–6
Cooking time: 18–20 minutes

1 lb (500 g) ground pork
1 onion, peeled and minced
1 teaspoon soy sauce
salt and pepper
1 small egg
dry breadcrumbs
oil for deep cooking

Mix the pork and onion together in a bowl, add soy sauce, salt and pepper. Beat the egg and add to the mixture, then form into small balls. Roll balls in breadcrumbs to coat evenly and chill for 30 minutes.
Heat oil in a wok or deep pan until hot, lower the pork balls into the hot oil, a few at a time, and cook for 4–5 minutes, until golden brown. Drain on paper towels and keep warm, until all the balls are cooked. Serve piping hot with a dipping sauce.

# Deep Fried Honey King Prawns

Serves: 4
Cooking time: 15–18 minutes

1 lb (500 g) fresh king prawns
flour
salt and pepper
oil for cooking

**Batter:**
3 tablespoons self-raising flour
½ teaspoon salt
½ teaspoon baking soda
1 egg, lightly beaten
3 tablespoons water

**Honey Sauce:**
2 teaspoons cornstarch
3 tablespoons chicken stock
1 tablespoon peanut oil
3 tablespoons honey
½ teaspoon salt

To make batter, sift flour, salt and soda into a bowl, add the beaten egg and gradually stir in water and mix until smooth.
Shell and de-vein the prawns and dust with flour, seasoned with salt and pepper. Heat oil in a wok or deep pan, dip prawns into the batter, one at a time, lower into the hot oil and cook for 4–5 minutes, until golden brown, lift out, drain on paper towels and keep warm.

For the sauce, blend cornstarch with chicken stock in a bowl until smooth. Heat peanut oil in a wok or pan and stir in cornstarch paste, add honey and salt and cook, stirring, until the sauce thickens. Serve prawns on warm plates after pouring the sauce over them.
(*Illustrated on page 70.*)

# Fondue Sin Sul Lo

Serves:  6
Cooking time:    20 minutes plus fondue

½ lb (250 g) pork steak
½ lb (250 g) beef steak
½ lb (250 g) veal steak
½ lb (250 g) sheep liver
½ lb (250 g) carrots
3 stalks celery
½ Chinese cabbage
4 cups (1 liter) water
1 teaspoon salt
2 cups long grain rice
parsley
1 tablespoon grated or prepared horseradish
1 tablespoon soy sauce
4–6 egg yolks

**Meat Broth:**
6 cups (1½ liters) water
6 beef bouillon cubes
2 onions, chopped
bouquet garni of parsley, thyme, and bay leaf
2 tablespoons sherry
2 cloves garlic, crushed.

Freeze the 4 meats slightly, until firm, then cut each into very thin slices. Wash vegetables, cut carrots into thin rings, celery into 1″ (2½ cm) lengths, cabbage into pieces and arrange meats and vegetables on a platter. Bring water to the boil in a pan, add salt and rice, reduce heat and cook for 20 minutes, without stirring.
Meanwhile, for the meat broth, combine water, beef cubes, onions and bouquet garni in a pan and boil for 5 minutes, reduce heat, cover and simmer for 15 minutes. Strain into another pan, add sherry and garlic and cook for 5 minutes. Transfer to the fondue and keep warm.
Remove rice from heat and allow to swell for 5

minutes, then spoon into small bowls and garnish with parsley. Place some horseradish into individual small bowls, add soy sauce, then an egg yolk to each bowl.
Cooking is done by each person using a fondue fork. Select meat and vegetable, lower into the hot broth and cook for 4–5 minutes, then lift out and dip into individual egg sauce bowl.
Meat broth soup is served last. Add any left over meat and or vegetables and rice, simmer and serve.

# Chicken Chow Mein

Serves:  4
Cooking time:    5–6 minutes

¾ lb (375 g) cooked chicken meat
1 onion
1 red bell pepper
1 stalk celery
4 scallions
1 cup of shredded Chinese cabbage
4 dried mushrooms, sliced
2 teaspoons light soy sauce
1 tablespoon dry sherry
3 teaspoons cornstarch
½ cup (125 ml) chicken stock
2 teaspoons peanut oil
2 slices root ginger, crushed
1 clove garlic, crushed
1 teaspoon salt
Crisp Fried Noodles — see recipe page 81

Cut chicken meat into bite size pieces. Cut onion into wedges, wash bell pepper, seed and slice, split celery in two and dice scallions into small pieces. Combine chicken, 1 teaspoon of soy sauce, sherry and 1 teaspoon cornstarch in a bowl, stir and marinate for 1 hour, stirring occasionally. Blend remaining cornstarch with chicken stock, until smooth.
Heat peanut oil in a wok pr pan, add ginger and garlic and stir-fry for 1 minute. Add chicken and marinade, onion, bell pepper, celery, scallions, cabbage and mushrooms and stir-fry for 1 minute. Mix salt, remaining soy sauce and cornstarch stock and add to the wok. Stir-fry for 1 minute, until mixture boils and thickens. Arrange noodles around the edge of warm plates, spoon chicken and vegetables in the center and serve hot.

▲ COD DUMPLINGS WITH MUSHROOMS (RECIPE PAGE 76)

▲ CHINESE NOODLES (RECIPE PAGE 76)

74

# Prawn Omelette

Serves:  4
Cooking time:  20–25 minutes

½ lb (250 g) cooked prawns, shelled
6 eggs
salt and pepper
4 scallions, finely chopped
1 slice root ginger, juiced
4 oz (125 g) bean sprouts
4 dried mushrooms, soaked and diced
pinch of glutamate
1 tablespoon peanut oil

### Sauce:
1 tablespoon cornstarch
½ cup (125 ml) chicken stock
2 teaspoons oyster sauce
1 teaspoon light soy sauce
1 teaspoon sugar
¼ teaspoon salt

To make the sauce, blend cornstarch and stock in a bowl, until smooth. Combine oyster and soy sauces, sugar and salt in a pan and stir in cornstarch blended stock. Heat, stirring, until sauce boils and thickens, then keep warm.

Break eggs into a bowl, season with salt and pepper and beat until slightly frothy, add scallions, ginger juice, bean sprouts, mushrooms, glutamate and prawns and mix well.

Barely cover the base of a wok or pan with oil and heat, add a quarter of the mixture and cook until slightly firm, turn over and cook, until lightly browned. Lift onto a warm plate and keep hot. Cook remaining 3 omelettes and serve with the sauce.

# Chinese Noodles

Serves: 4–6
Cooking time: 8–10 minutes

    4–6 bundles of egg noodles
    4 dried mushrooms
    1 green bell pepper
    1 leek
    1 carrot
    ¼ lb (125 g) bean sprouts
    2½ tablespoons oil
    ½ teaspoon salt
    pinch of pepper
    1 tablespoon soy sauce
    4 tablespoons chicken stock

Soak, boil, drain and dry noodles as for Boiled Noodles — see recipe page 86. Soak mushrooms in hot water for 20 minutes, drain and pat dry, discard stems and slice caps into quarters. Wash and seed bell pepper and cut into strips. Wash leek and chop into 1″ (2½ cm) lengths. Cut carrot into thin strips. Rinse, drain and slice bean sprouts. Heat 2 teaspoons of oil in a wok or pan, add bean sprouts and cook for 2 minutes, remove sprouts and set aside. Add remaining oil to the wok and heat. Add mushrooms, bell pepper, leek and carrot and stir-fry for 1 minute. Add noodles, bean sprouts, salt and pepper and sprinkle with soy sauce. Toss well, until noodles are coated. Add chicken stock, stir until well blended and serve. (Illustrated on page 74.)

# Chicken Wings

Serves: 4
Cooking time: 35–40 minutes

    1 lb (500 g) chicken wings
    2 chicken stock cubes
    2 tablespoons oyster sauce
    1 clove garlic, crushed
    1 teaspoon soy sauce
    1 cup (250 ml) chicken stock
    1 slice of root ginger, crushed
    1 teaspoon sugar
    salt and pepper to taste

Place chicken wings in a pan with enough water to cover and add crumbled stock cubes, bring to the boil, cover and simmer for 12 minutes, then drain. Combine oyster sauce, garlic, soy sauce, chicken stock, ginger, sugar and the chicken wings in a wok or pan and bring to the boil, reduce heat and simmer for 20 minutes. Spoon onto warm plates, sprinkle with salt and pepper to taste and serve.

# Cod Dumplings with Mushrooms

Serves: 4–6
Cooking time: 15–18 minutes

    1 lb (500 g) cod fillets
    8 dried mushrooms
    1 teaspoon glutamate
    2 tablespoons light soy sauce
    juice of 1 lemon
    1 tablespoon cornstarch
    ¼ cup dry, soft breadcrumbs
    1 tablespoon flour
    1 egg, well beaten
    2 cups (500 ml) water
    2 tablespoons oil
    2 medium onions, sliced

**Sauce:**
    3 tablespoons tomato catsup
    3 tablespoons wine vinegar
    5 tablespoons sugar
    2 tablespoons cornstarch

For the sauce, combine all ingredients in a pan and cook, stirring constantly, for 2–3 minutes, until sauce thickens.
Rinse and dry fish, cut into cubes and place in a bowl. Soak mushrooms in water for 1 hour. Mix glutamate, soy sauce and lemon juice together and pour over the fish, baste and leave to marinate for 20 minutes, then mash the fish and marinade until smooth. Add cornstarch, breadcrumbs, flour and egg and mix well, then form into small dumplings. Bring water to the boil in a pan and add dumplings, reduce heat, cover and simmer gently, do not boil, for 6–7 minutes. Meanwhile, drain mushrooms and pat dry. Heat oil in a wok or pan until hot, add

onions and stir-fry for 1–2 minutes, until golden brown. Add mushrooms and cook for 1 minute. Remove onions and mushrooms and keep warm. Lift out dumplings and drain for 1 minute, place on warm plates with mushrooms and onions on top and serve with the sauce.
*(Illustrated on page 74.)*

# Pork and Almonds

Serves: 4
Cooking time: 15–18 minutes

¾ lb (375 g) lean pork
4 oz (125 g) blanched almonds
1 tablespoon butter
6 oz (190 g) can button mushrooms
4 oz (100 g) can baby corn
8 oz (230 g) can bamboo shoots
1 stalk celery
1 cup frozen peas
2 teaspoons cornstarch
½ teaspoon salt
½ teaspoon glutamate
1 teaspoon soy sauce
1 tablespoon water
2 tablespoons oil
1 cup (250 ml) chicken stock

Dice the pork. Split the almonds in half, into a small pan. Add butter and cook over low heat, until almonds are lightly tinted, then set pan aside. Drain mushrooms, corn and bamboo shoots and cut shoots finely. Cut celery, diagonally, into 1″ (2½ cm) pieces and defrost the peas. Mix cornstarch, salt, glutamate, soy sauce and water in a bowl until blended.
Heat oil in a wok or pan, add pork and stir-fry for 1 minute, add mushrooms, corn, bamboo shoots, celery and peas and stir-fry for 2 minutes. Stir in stock and cornstarch mixture and bring to the boil, stirring. Reduce heat, cover and simmer for 5–6 minutes. Re-heat the almonds. Serve the pork and sauce on warm plates and sprinkle with almonds.

# Pork Savouries

Serves: 4–6
Cooking time: 12–15 minutes

½ lb (250 g) pork flank
1 egg
1 stalk, celery, finely chopped
2 scallions, finely chopped
1 teaspoon salt
4 slices of stale bread
oil for deep cooking

Grind the pork and combine with egg, celery, scallions and salt in a bowl and mix well. Cut crusts from the bread and discard. Spread the mixture thickly over the bread, then cut into small squares. Heat oil in a deep pan, add the bread squares, a few at a time, and cook for 2–3 minutes, until golden brown. Drain on absorbent paper and keep warm, until all squares are cooked. Serve hot or cold.

# Fried Spinach

Serves: 4
Cooking time: 6–7 minutes

1 bunch of spinach
2 tablespoons peanut oil
1 clove garlic, crushed
½ teaspoon salt
1 teaspoon sugar
1 tablespoon soy sauce
juice of 1 lemon

Wash the spinach, remove stalks and slice the leaves. Cut two of the spinach stalks into 1″ (2½ cm) diagonal pieces.
Heat oil in a wok or pan, add garlic and cook for 30 seconds, add spinach stalks and leaves and stir-fry to coat with oil. Add salt, sugar and soy sauce and stir well. Add lemon juice, stir and cook for 2 minutes, then serve immediately.

## Vermicelli Soup with Mushrooms

Serves: 4–6
Cooking time: 35–40 minutes

½ lb (250 g) beef soup bone
6 cup (1½ liters) water
1 teaspoon salt
dash of pepper
6 dried mushrooms
1 small onion, finely chopped
2 spring onions, cut into 1″ (2½ cm) lengths
4 oz (125 g) bean sprouts
1 teaspoon oyster sauce
2 small bunches vermicelli noodles

Cut meat into very thin strips and place in a large pan with water, salt and pepper and bring to the boil. Reduce heat, cover and simmer for 20 minutes. Meanwhile, soak mushrooms in hot water for 18–20 minutes, drain, discard stems and cut caps into halves. Drain bean sprouts, wash and drain again.
Add mushroom, onion, spring onions, bean sprouts and oyster sauce to the pan, cover and simmer for 10–12 minutes. Add vermicelli noodles and simmer for 2–3 minutes.

# Chicken Noodle Soup

Serves: 4–6
Cooking time: 10–12 minutes

½ lb (250 g) leftover cooked chicken meat
2 slices ham
6 cups (1½ liters) Basic Chicken Stock — see
   recipe page 86
1 small bundle of fine noodles
1 teaspoon soy sauce
12 stalks Chinese choy sim or scallions
salt to taste.

Cut chicken meat into small pieces and slice ham into thin strips. Combine chicken stock and pieces in a large pan and bring to the boil, reduce heat and simmer for 3–4 minutes. Add noodles, soy sauce, choy sim and salt to taste and simmer for 2–3 minutes. Lift out choy sim and arrange around each bowl, add soup, sprinkle with ham strips and serve hot.

# Crab Salad

Serves: 4

8 oz (440 g) can crabmeat
8 oz (250 g) bean sprouts
14 oz (425 g) can hearts of palm
6 dried mushrooms
1 sprig of coriander, finely chopped, (or ½
    teaspoon dried coriander)
1 tablespoon salad oil
1 teaspoon sesame oil
2 teaspoons ice water
2 teaspoons lemon juice
pinch of salt
dash of pepper
¼ teaspoon garlic paste
sprig of mint for garnish

Drain crabmeat and break into small pieces, drain bean sprouts and hearts of palm. Soak mushrooms in hot water for 20 minutes, drain and pat dry, discard stems and chop caps in halves. Place crabmeat, bean sprouts, hearts of palm, mushrooms and coriander in a salad bowl, cover and chill for 1 hour.
In a jar, combine salad and sesame oils, ice water, lemon juice, salt, pepper with garlic paste, cover lightly, shake vigorously, then chill 1 hour. Shake dressing and pour over salad, toss gently, garnish with mint and serve.
(Illustrated on page 79.)

# Fish Balls, Poached or Fried

Serves: 4–6
Cooking time:    Fried 4–5 minutes
                 Poached 5–6 minutes

1 lb (500 g) fish fillets (whiting, flounder or
    similar)
3 scallions
1 small egg
1 teaspoon cornstarch
1 thin slice of root ginger, crushed
½ teaspoon salt
1 tablespoon lemon juice
Sweet and Sour Sauce — see recipe page 90

Skin and bone the fish and mince. Chop scallions finely and beat egg well. Combine fish, scallions, egg, cornstarch, ginger, salt and lemon juice in a dish and mix until blended and very smooth. Form into small 1″ (2½ cm) balls and chill for 30 minutes. For poaching, bring 6 cups (1½ liter) of water to the boil, reduce heat a little and drop in fish balls. Poach for 5–6 minutes, then remove with a slotted spoon and drain.
For frying, coat fish balls well with cornstarch and cook in a deep pan of hot oil for 4–5 minutes, until golden brown, then remove and drain on absorbent paper.
Serve fish balls hot on warm plates with Sweet and Sour Sauce.

# Pork and Bean Curd Soup

Serves: 4
Cooking time:    20–25 minutes

¼ lb (125 g) lean pork
3 dried mushrooms
1 small carrot
1 Chinese cabbage leaf
2 pieces of bean curd
2 drops sesame oil
salt and pepper
¼ teaspoon glutamate
6 cups (1½ liters) chicken stock
2 scallions

Finely slice the pork. Soak mushrooms in hot water for 20 minutes and drain, discard stems and cut caps into quarters. Scrape the carrot and cut into thin rings, shred the cabbage leaf, cut the bean curd into 1″ (2½ cm) pieces. Combine pork with sesame oil, salt, pepper and glutamate in a bowl and mix well.
Bring stock to the boil in a large pan, add carrot and mushrooms, reduce heat, cover and simmer until tender, add cabbage and cook for 1 minute. Add pork mixture and cook for 15 minutes, over gentle heat, add bean curd and cook for ½ a minute. Serve immediately, sprinkled with finely chopped scallions.

# Lemon Chicken

Serves: 4–6
Cooking time: 12 minutes

*8 chicken pieces*
*½ cup cornstarch*
*3 tablespoons water*
*2 egg yolks, beaten*
*salt and pepper*
*flour*
*oil for deep cooking*
*4 scallions, finely chopped*
*Lemon Sauce — see recipe page 90*

Bone and skin the chicken pieces and cut into bite size pieces. Place cornstarch in a bowl and gradually stir in water, beaten egg yolks, salt and pepper and mix into a thin, smooth batter. Roll chicken in flour, dip into the batter, then cook in a deep pan of hot oil, a few pieces at a time, until golden brown. Lift out with a slotted spoon, and drain on paper towels. Serve on warm plates, sprinkled with scallions, with hot Lemon Sauce.

# Curried Prawns

Serves: 4
Cooking time: 10 minutes

*1 lb (500 g) cooked prawns or shrimp*
*2 medium onions*
*3 teaspoons cornstarch*
*1 cup (250 ml) chicken stock*
*3 teaspoons peanut oil*
*1 clove garlic, crushed*
*1–2 teaspoons curry, to taste*
*¼ teaspoon salt*
*¼ teaspoon glutamate*
*1 teaspoon soy sauce*
*Boiled Rice — see recipe page 86*

Shell and de-vein the prawns, rinse and pat dry. Peel onions and cut into thin wedges. Blend cornstarch with chicken stock in a bowl.
Heat peanut oil in a wok or pan, add garlic and stir-fry for one minute, add onions and stir-fry for 1–2 minutes, until transparent. Add curry powder and stir well over low heat for 2 minutes. Stir in salt, glutamate, soy sauce, cornstarch stock and prawns and simmer, stirring, for 5 minutes. Serve with Boiled Rice.

# Eggs in Soy Sauce

Serves: 4
Cooking time: 12–15 minutes

*4 eggs*
*boiling water*
*3 tablespoons soy sauce*
*½ teaspoon sugar*
*3 tablespoons water*
*½ teaspoon sesame oil*

Cook eggs in a pan of boiling water for 5 minutes and drain. Allow eggs to become cold, then shell. Combine soy sauce, sugar, water and sesame oil in a pan and bring to the boil, add eggs, reduce heat and simmer for 10 minutes. Set pan aside until cold, then lift out eggs, cut into quarters and serve.

# Crisp Fried Noodles

Serves: allow 1 bundle per person
Cooking time: 2–3 minutes per bundle

*16 oz (454 g) packet (10 bundles) fine noodles*
*oil for deep frying*

Soak, drain and dry noodles as for Soft Fried Noodles. Heat oil in a deep pan to high heat, add noodles, 1 bundle at a time, and cook 2–3 minutes, until golden brown. Lift out, drain well on absorbent paper and serve.
Or, add noodles to an oiled pan, cook and press against the pan base, with a spatula, until slightly browned. Turn with a spatula and brown. Lift out and serve.

# Barbecued Spareribs

Serves: 4–6
Cooking time: 1 hour
Oven: 190°C increase to 230°C
375°F increase to 450°F

2 lbs (1 kg) pork spareribs
1 clove garlic, crushed
2 thin slices of root ginger, crushed
1 teaspoon sugar
1 tablespoon hoi sin sauce
2 tablespoons light soy sauce
2 tablespoons white vinegar
2 tablespoons honey
2 tablespoons sherry
2 tablespoons bacon cube stock
Plum Sauce — see recipe page 89

Trim fat from pork and cut ribs in half. Combine garlic, ginger, sugar, hoi sin sauce, soy sauce, vinegar, honey, sherry and stock in a bowl and mix well, add spareribs, baste and set aside to marinate for 4 hours. Lift ribs from marinade and place on a rack in a pan containing a little water and cook in a moderately hot oven for 45 minutes. Increase the heat to very hot and cook 15 minutes. Meanwhile, pour marinade into a pan and cook, stirring for 2–3 minutes. Serve spareribs with heated marinade and Plum Sauce.

# Honeyed Chicken

Serves: 6–8
Cooking time: 10–12 minutes

4 whole chicken breasts
½ lb (250 g) ground lean pork
1 lb (500 g) fresh shrimp, shelled and finely
    chopped
1 stalk celery, finely chopped
6 scallions, chopped
1 teaspoon soy sauce
1 tablespoon sherry
1 piece green ginger, crushed
flour
1 egg, beaten
2 tablespoons milk
dry breadcrumbs
oil for deep cooking

**Honey Sauce:**
1 tablespoon cornstarch
1 cup (250 ml) chicken stock
½ cup (125 ml) tomato catsup
4 tablespoons honey
1 teaspoon soy sauce
2 tablespoons dry sherry
2 tablespoons white vinegar

For the sauce, blend cornstarch with chicken stock. Mix catsup, honey, soy sauce, sherry and vinegar together in a pan. Stir in cornstarch stock and bring to the boil, reduce heat and simmer for 2–3 minutes.
Cut chicken breasts in half and remove bones and skin, to give 8 pieces of chicken. Pound chicken until thin. Combine pork, shrimp, celery, scallions, soy sauce, sherry and ginger in a bowl and mix well. Press mixture evenly over the chicken pieces and coat with flour. Dip in beaten egg mixed with milk, then coat with breadcrumbs.
Cook chicken in a deep pan of hot oil (not overly hot) for 3–4 minutes, until golden brown. Lift out and drain on absorbent paper. Cut chicken into 1" (2½ cm) slices and serve on warm plates with Honey Sauce spooned on top.

# Chinese Beef with Bean Sprouts

Serves: 4–6
Cooking time: 10–12 minutes

1 lb (500 g) lean beef
1 medium onion
1 red bell pepper
8 oz (250 g) bean sprouts
2 teaspoons cornstarch
1 tablespoon water
2 tablespoons oil
1 clove garlic, crushed
1 thin slice root ginger, crushed
2 teaspoons soy sauce
2 tablespoons dry sherry
½ teaspoon glutamate
1 teaspoon sugar
salt and pepper to taste
⅔ cup (165 ml) beef stock
Boiled Rice — see recipe page 86

Trim meat and cut into 2½" (5 cm) strips. Peel onion and cut into rings. Wash bell pepper, seed and cut into chunks. Drain bean sprouts. Blend cornstarch with water to a paste.

Heat 1 tablespoon of oil in a wok or pan, over medium heat, add meat and stir-fry for 2 minutes, lift out and drain. Add remaining oil to the wok and heat, add onion, garlic and ginger and stir-fry for 1 minute. Stir in soy sauce, sherry and bell pepper and stir-fry for 2 minutes. Add glutamate, sugar, salt, pepper and stock and stir. Return meat to the wok, add bean sprouts and blended cornstarch, stirring constantly, until mixture thickens. Reduce heat, cover, and simmer for 2 minutes, Serve on warm plates with Boiled Rice.

# Sweet and Sour Chinese Drumsticks

Serves:  4–6
Cooking time:  15 minutes

*6 chicken drumsticks*
*1 egg*
*1 tablespoon milk*
*4 tablespoons cornstarch*
*pinch salt and pepper*
*1 medium onion*
*1 small green bell pepper*
*1 medium carrot*
*1 piece syruped or preserved ginger, chopped in*
  *wedges*
*1 tablespoon light soy sauce*
*3 tablespoons tomato sauce*
*2 tablespoons malt vinegar*
*1 tablespoon sherry*
*1 tablespoon cornstarch, extra*
*2 tablespoons sugar*
*1 cup (250 ml) water*
*oil for deep cooking*

Trim and wipe the drumsticks. Beat the egg with milk. Mix cornstarch with salt and pepper. Cut the onion into thin wedges. Remove seeds from bell pepper and cut into chunks. Scrape carrot and cut into thin rings.

Drop these vegetables into a pan of boiling water and cook for 5 minutes, drain well, then put aside with the ginger. Mix together in a pan, soy sauce, tomato sauce, vinegar, sherry, extra cornstarch, sugar and water and bring to the boil, stirring constantly, reduce heat and simmer for 2–3 minutes, for the sauce.

Dip drumsticks into the egg mixture, then cover well in cornstarch and cook in a deep pan (or deep fryer to 180°C–350°F) of hot oil, not over hot, for 10 minutes, until golden and tender. Drain on paper towels and keep warm. Re-heat sauce, add vegetables and ginger, stir for 1 minute. Arrange drumsticks on warm plates, pour sauce over them, garnish with parsley and serve at once.

# Beef in Oyster Sauce

Serves:  4
Cooking time:  6–8 minutes

*1 lb (500 g) rump or top round steak*
*salt and pepper*
*2 tablespoons peanut oil*
*1 clove garlic, crushed*
*1 piece of root ginger, crushed*
*1 egg white, beaten*
*3 tablespoons oyster sauce*
*1 tablespoon beef stock*
*1 teaspoon soy sauce*
*1 teaspoon sherry*
*½ teaspoon glutamate*
*1 teaspoon sesame oil*
*1 medium onion*
*Vermicelli — Transparent Noodles — see recipe*
  *page 32*
*Fluffy Rice — see recipe page 37*

Slice beef against the grain into small, thin pieces, pound gently with a mallet and sprinkle with salt and pepper. Combine 2 teaspoons of oil, garlic, ginger and egg white in a bowl and mix well, add the meat, baste and marinate for 1 hour. In a bowl, mix oyster sauce, stock, soy sauce, sherry, glutamate and sesame oil together for the sauce. Cut onion into wedges.

Heat remaining oil in a wok or pan, add onion and stir-fry, until transparent, then lift out. Add meat and marinade to the wok and stir-fry, until meat is lightly browned. Return onion to the wok, stir in sauce and stir-fry for 3–4 minutes. Serve hot on warm plates surrounded by Transparent Noodles or Fluffy Rice.

# Drawn Thread Apples

Serves: 4
Cooking time: 10–12 minutes

    4 apples
    3 tablespoons flour
    3 teaspoons cornstarch
    1 egg white, beaten
    oil for deep cooking
    ½ cup sugar
    3 tablespoons water
    1 tablespoon peanut oil

Peel and core the apples, and cut each into 8 pieces and roll in flour. Combine leftover flour with cornstarch and egg white and mix until smooth, add apple pieces and coat well.
Heat oil in a deep pan and when hot, add apple pieces and cook for 3–4 minutes, until golden. Drain well on absorbent paper.
Heat sugar and water in a wok or pan until sugar is dissolved and mixture is tacky, add peanut oil and cook until hot, add apple pieces and baste to cover with the sauce. Spoon the hot apples into a warm, greased bowl and using chopsticks, lift apple pieces, one at a time, with the molten threads hanging, plunge into a bowl of iced water to harden the glaze, and serve.

# Beef in Black Bean Sauce

Serves: 4–6
Cooking time: 10–12 minutes

    1 lb (500 g) lean beef
    2 tablespoons black beans
    2 cloves garlic, crushed
    ½ teaspoon salt
    2 tablespoons dry sherry
    ¼ cup beef stock
    2 teaspoons soy sauce
    1 medium onion
    1 tablespoon cornstarch
    3 tablespoons water
    4 tablespoons oil
    2 teaspoons sugar

Pound beef until thin, discard any fat, and cut meat into thin strips 2″ (5 cm) long. Soak black beans in a bowl of cold water for 30 minutes, then drain, rinse and pound to a paste in a small bowl, with garlic. Combine meat with salt, sherry, stock and soy sauce in a bowl and baste well. Place bowl on the lowest shelf of fridge to marinate for 1 hour. Cut onion into thin slices. Blend cornstarch with water to a thin paste. Drain meat, but reserve marinade. Heat 3 tablespoons of oil in a wok or pan, add meat and stir-fry over high heat for 1 minute, until brown, then lift out. Add onion to the wok and stir-fry for 1 minute, until transparent, then lift out. Add remaining oil to the wok and cook bean paste, stirring, for 1 minute. Stir in sugar, reserved marinade and blended cornstarch and stir-fry for 1 minute, Return meat and onion to the wok, stir well and cook for 2 minutes. Serve immediately.

# Marinated Red Roast Pork

Serves: 4
Cooking time: 45–50 minutes
Oven:   220°C reduce to 180°C
        425°F reduce to 350°F

    1½ lbs (750 g) pork roast
    peanut oil
    a few grains of Chinese red powder
    8 tablespoons chicken stock
    3 teaspoons cornstarch
    2 tablespoons water
    Fluffy Rice — see recipe page 37

**Marinade:**
    1 clove garlic, crushed
    2 thin slices root ginger, crushed
    2 teaspoons sugar
    1 teaspoon five spice powder
    1 tablespoon honey
    1 tablespoon hoi sin sauce
    2 tablespoons light soy sauce
    ½ cup dry sherry

Combine all ingredients for the marinade in a dish and mix until smooth.
Trim the pork of any fat, brush with oil and place in the marinade, baste well and set aside to marinate

for 2 hours, basting occasionally. Lift out pork, but reserve the marinade, brush meat again with oil and place on a rack in a baking dish.

Cook in a pre-heated very hot oven for 10 minutes, then reduce heat to moderate, brush pork with marinade and cook a further 30—35 minutes, brushing pork again with marinade, 15 minutes before cooking is completed. Place pork on a carving dish and allow to rest in a warm place for 10 minutes. Remove rack, stir a few grains of red powder into the pan drippings, add chicken stock and marinade and cook over medium heat, stirring until boiling. Blend cornstarch with water and stir into the gravy to thicken. Slice pork diagonally and serve on Fluffy Rice and spoon the gravy over the top.

# Pork with Sweet and Sour Sauce

Serves:  4
Cooking time:   18—20 minutes

1 lb (500 g) lean pork
1 tablespoon sugar
1 tablespoon soy sauce
2 tablespoons sherry
2 tablespoons chicken stock
1 egg
4 tablespoons cornstarch
oil for deep cooking

**Sauce:**
1 medium onion
1 medium carrot
boiling salted water
2 stalks celery
½ green bell pepper
2 canned pineapple rings, chopped
2 teaspoons cornstarch
1 tablespoon water
3 tablespoons vinegar
1½ tablespoons sugar
2 teaspoons soy sauce
½ teaspoon salt
1 cup chicken stock
2 pieces syruped or preserved ginger, finely
   sliced

Cut pork into 1″ (2½ cm) cubes. Combine sugar, soy sauce, sherry and stock in a bowl and mix well, add the pork and baste, then set aside to marinate for 1 hour, basting occasionally.

For the sauce, peel onion and cut into thin wedges. Scrape the carrot, cut into thin strips and par-boil in boiling salted water for 2 minutes, then drain. Slice celery, diagonally, into small pieces. Seed bell pepper and chop coarsely. Blend cornstarch with water into a smooth paste.

Mix sugar and vinegar in a wok or pan and stir over low heat until sugar is dissolved. Add soy sauce, salt, stock, onion, celery, carrot, pineapple and bell pepper and simmer for 2 minutes. Stir in blended cornstarch and stir until boiling, add ginger and simmer for 2 minutes, then keep warm.

Beat egg lightly in a bowl, gradually stir in corn-starch, until blended and smooth, then add drained pork pieces and stir to coat well.

Heat the oil in a wok or deep pan until hot, add pork pieces, a few at a time, and cook until golden brown. Lift out and drain on paper towels and keep warm, until all the pork is cooked. Place pork on warm plates, pour the sauce on top and serve immediately.

# Hot Chili Prawns

Serves:  4
Cooking time:   8—10 minutes

1½ lbs (750 g) fresh prawns or shrimp
1 teaspoon crushed root ginger
4 cloves garlic, crushed
2 spring onions, chopped finely
2 dried chili peppers
½ teaspoon salt
6 tablespoons peanut oil
1 cup (250 ml) chicken stock
2 tablespoons light soy sauce
Boiled Rice — see recipe page 86

Shell the prawns, and wash under running water, dry well and sprinkle with salt. Break the chillies into small pieces. Heat oil in a wok or pan and when hot, add prawns and stir-fry for 1 minute. Add ginger, garlic, onions and chillies and stir-fry for 2 minutes. Pour stock and soy sauce over the prawns and stir-fry until liquid is nearly evaporated. Serve immediately with Boiled Rice.

# Spring Roll Wrappers

Makes 25–30 wrappers

> 2 cups flour
> 1½ cups (375 ml) water

Sift the flour into a bowl and gradually add water, stirring until a well mixed batter. Heat a 6″ or 8″ (15 cm or 20 cm) frying pan over very low heat and grease with an oil soaked cloth. Add about 1 tablespoon of batter, tilt and rotate pan to spread batter evenly over the base and cook until a dry, paper thin pancake, then turn out on to a flat dish. Repeat the process with the remainder of the batter. Use waxed paper between wrappers to prevent sticking.

# Boiled Rice

Serves: 4
Cooking time: 25 minutes

> 1 cup rice
> 2 cups water
> 1 teaspoon salt

Wash rice under cold running water, in a sieve, until water runs clear, to remove excess dust and starch. Add water and salt to a large pot and bring to the boil, add rice, then reduce heat slightly, stir rice once, replace lid tightly, simmer 30 minutes; and serve hot.

# Basic Chicken Stock

Cooking time: 2–2¼ hours

> 1 large chicken
> cold water
> 1 teaspoon salt
> 1 onion, peeled and quartered
> 1 stalk of celery with leaves, chopped
> 2 carrots, peeled and diced
> 2 thin slices of fresh root ginger
> 2 tablespoons sherry
> 3 sprigs of parsley

Place chicken in a deep pan with water, add salt and bring to the boil, cover and simmer gently for 1½ hours. Lift out chicken and bone, (save the meat for other dishes). Return neck and bones to the pan. Add onion, celery, carrots, ginger, sherry and parsley and bring to the boil. Reduce heat, cover and simmer for 30 minutes, skimming occasionally. Strain the stock through a sieve, then through muslin, into a bowl, cool and chill overnight. Skim any fat from the surface, then store, covered, in a refrigerator or freezer, until needed. Makes about 8 cups (2 liters) of stock.

# Boiled Noodles

Serves: Allow 1 bundle per person
Cooking time: fine noodles 2–3 minutes per bundle
wide noodles 3–4 minutes per bundle

> 16 oz (454 g) packet (10 bundles) noodles
> water
> 1 tablespoon peanut oil

Soak noodles in a bowl of hot water for 8–10 minutes, separating the strands, then drain. Bring a large pan of water to the boil and add oil. Drop noodles into the pan, return water to the boil and cook fine noodles for 2–3 minutes, or wide noodles for 3–4 minutes. Noodles should be firm but tender; do not overcook. Drain noodles and rinse off excess starch under running hot water.

# Hong Kong Prawn Balls

Serves: 4
Cooking time: 12–15 minutes

> 1 lb (500 g) fresh king prawns or shrimp
> flour
> salt and pepper
> oil for deep cooking
> Vermicelli — Transparent Noodles — see recipe page 32

**Batter:**
*3 tablespoons self-raising flour*
*½ teaspoon salt*
*½ teaspoon bicarbonate of soda*
*1 egg*
*3 tablespoons water*

For the batter, sift flour, salt and soda into a bowl, add egg and mix, gradually add water, stirring into a smooth batter. Cover with a cloth and set aside for 15 minutes.

Shell and de-vein the prawns, chop into 1″ (2½ cm) pieces, form into balls and roll in flour, seasoned with salt and pepper. Dip prawn balls in batter to cover well and cook in a deep pan of hot oil, a few at a time, until crisp and golden. Lift out and drain on paper towels and keep hot. Arrange noodles on a warm platter, add hot prawn balls and serve with a dipping sauce.

# Sweet and Sour Prawns

Serves:   4
Cooking time:   6−8 minutes

*1 lb (500 g) cooked prawns*
*salt and pepper to taste*
*1 tablespoon dry sherry*
*1 onion*
*1 green bell pepper*
*2 canned pineapple rings*
*½ cup sugar*
*2 thin slices of green ginger, crushed*
*½ cup (125 ml) vinegar*
*2 teaspoons light soy sauce*
*2 tablespoons extra sherry*
*2 tablespoons tomato sauce*
*2 tablespoons cornstarch*
*½ cup (125 ml) water*
*1 tablespoon peanut oil*

Shell and de-vein the prawns, rinse and pat dry, place in a bowl and sprinkle with salt, pepper and sherry, mix well and set aside to marinate for 30 minutes. Peel onion and cut into thin wedges, seed the bell pepper and cut into small chunks, and cut pineapple rings into wedges.

Combine sugar, ginger, vinegar, soy sauce, extra sherry and tomato sauce in a bowl, mix well and set aside for the sauce. Blend cornstarch with water in a bowl to a smooth paste.

Heat oil in a wok or pan, add onion and bell pepper and stir-fry for 1−2 minutes, add the sauce mixture and stir-fry for 1−2 minutes. Add prawns, pineapple and blended cornstarch and bring to the boil, stirring constantly, until the mixture thickens. Reduce heat and simmer for 2 minutes. Serve hot.

# Hot Ice Cream Balls

Serves:   8−10
Cooking time:   2−3 minutes

*2 quarts of full cream vanilla*
*  ice cream, first quality*
*3 tablespoons gelatin*
*6 tablespoons water*
*2 eggs*
*4 tablespoons milk*
*flour*
*dry breadcrumbs*
*oil for deep cooking*
*cocktail sticks*

Chill 2 oven trays and a medium ice cream scoop in the freezer. Spoon ice cream into a bowl to soften a little, but do not melt. Dissolve gelatin in cold water over a pan of simmering water, stirring. When cool, add to the ice cream and beat until blended and smooth, using an electric mixer. Place bowl in the freezer for 8 hours or overnight, until hard frozen. Scoop balls of ice cream and place on chilled trays, inserting a cocktail stick in each ball, return trays to the freezer, until balls are hard.

Meanwhile, beat eggs in a bowl and gradually stir in milk, until blended. Place breadcrumbs and flour in separate bowls. Working swiftly and using cocktail sticks to handle, coat each ball in flour, then dip in egg mixture and coat with breadcrumbs, return to the trays, carefully removing cocktail sticks and freeze until hard.

Heat oil in a deep pan, when hot, add ice cream balls, a couple at a time, and cook for approximately ½ minute, until golden. Lift out balls, drain on paper towels and serve immediately with warmed strawberry, caramel or chocolate sauce.

# Honey Prawns

Serves: 4
Cooking time: 8–10 minutes

1½ lbs (750 g) fresh prawns
3 tablespoons cornstarch
½ teaspoon salt
dash of pepper
3 teaspoons extra cornstarch
1 tablespoon chicken stock
3 tablespoons oil
3 tablespoons honey
Fried Rice — see recipe page

Shell and de-vein the prawns, rinse and pat dry, dust with the 2 tablespoons of cornstarch, seasoned with salt and pepper. Blend extra cornstarch with chicken stock in a small bowl, until smooth. Heat oil in a wok or pan until very hot, add prawns and cook for 2 minutes, until golden, stirring often. Stir in blended cornstarch and cook until slightly thickened, stir in honey and heat, stirring to coat prawns well. Serve hot with Fried Rice.

# Crisp Skin Chicken

Serves: 6
Cooking time: 45–50 minutes

3 lbs (1½ kg) chicken
1 teaspoon salt
1 piece anise
4 peppercorns
1 small onion, chopped
1 stalk celery, chopped
2 tablespoons honey
1 tablespoon vinegar
2 teaspoons light soy sauce
2 tablespoons sherry
salt and pepper
3 tablespoons cornstarch
6 cups (1½ liters) oil
Fried Salt and Pepper Mix — see recipe page 91

Place chicken in a large pan and pour in boiling water to reach halfway up the side of the bird, add salt, anise, peppercorns, onion and celery and bring to the boil, reduce heat and simmer for 20 minutes. Remove pan from heat and allow chicken to become cool in the liquid. Lift out the chicken, drain and pat dry on paper towels, then place in a shallow dish.

In a small bowl, combine honey, vinegar, soy sauce, sherry, salt and pepper and mix well, then pour over the chicken and set aside to marinate for 1 hour, turning frequently and brushing with marinade over all parts of the bird. Lift chicken from marinade and place on a rack over a tray and chill on lowest shelf of refrigerator for 8 hours or overnight. Lift out chicken and allow to come to room temperature, dust well with cornstarch and leave for 10 minutes.

Heat oil in a deep pan (or deep fryer, 180°C, 350°F), add chicken and cook until crisp and golden brown, basting continually. Lift out chicken, drain well on paper towels and cut into serving pieces. Arrange chicken on warm plates, sprinkle fried salt and pepper around the edge and serve immediately. Provide lemon water and plenty of paper napkins, as this dish is eaten with the fingers.

# Mandarin Duck

Serves: 6
Cooking time: 35–40 minutes

4 lbs (2 kg) dressed duck
2 pieces syruped ginger, finely chopped
1 teaspoon salt
dash of pepper
3 tablespoons dry sherry
⅔ cup (165 ml) chicken stock
3 large, juicy mandarins
1 tablespoon cornstarch
4 tablespoons water
3 tablespoons soy sauce
2 teaspoons sugar
½ cup (125 ml) red wine
1 teaspoon Hoi Sin Jeong sauce
extra cornstarch
4 tablespoons oil

Wash duck thoroughly, dry well and discard neck and giblets. Chop in half and carefully remove bones, then cut meat into 12 pieces. Combine duck pieces with ginger, salt, pepper, sherry and chicken stock in a large bowl, stir gently and set aside to marinate for 2 hours.

Squeeze the juice from one mandarin and reserve two pieces of the peel. Peel remaining mandarins and break into segments. Blend cornstarch with water in a bowl until smooth.

Lift out duck pieces and drain. Pour marinade into a pan with soy sauce, sugar, wine, Hoi Sin Jeong sauce, mandarin peel and juice and set aside. Dust duck pieces well with extra cornstarch.

Heat oil in a wok or pan over medium heat, add duck, 3–4 pieces at a time, and stir-fry for 4–5 minutes, lift out, drain and place in a flameproof casserole dish, cover and keep warm.

Heat pan with marinade and mandarin mixture and bring to the boil, reduce heat and simmer for 3–4 minutes, stirring constantly, then pour over the duck and baste. Place casserole over heat and simmer for 10–12 minutes. Discard mandarin peel, then stir in cornstarch mixture until thickened. Serve duck on warm plates and garnish with mandarin segments.

# Gow Gees

Serves: 4–6
Cooking time: 12–15 minutes

*½ lb (250 g) lean pork*
*6 oz (185 g) fresh prawns or shrimp*
*6 dried mushrooms*
*hot water*
*6 scallions, finely chopped*
*8 oz (250 g) bamboo shoots, finely chopped*
*2 slices green ginger, crushed*
*1 teaspoon sugar*
*1 tablespoon dry sherry*
*1 teaspoon soy sauce*
*1 teaspoon sesame oil*
*30 Gow Gee or Wonton Wrappers — see recipe*
 *page 63*
*egg white or water*
*Plum Sauce — see recipe this page*
*Sweet ad Sour Sauce — see recipe page 90*

Grind the pork. Shell and de-vein prawns and grind finely. Soak mushrooms in hot water for 30 minutes and drain, discard stems and chop caps

finely. Combine pork, prawns and mushrooms in a bowl with scallions, bamboo shoots, ginger, sugar, sherry, soy sauce and sesame oil and mix thoroughly.

Spread out Gow Gee Wrappers (Wonton Wrappers are cut with a 3″ (7½ cm) cutter into circles) and place a rounded teaspoon of mixture on the center of each wrapper, brush edges with egg white or water and fold wrappers over filling to make half circles, pinch to seal. Place Gow Gees in a steamer over boiling water, cover and steam for 12–15 minutes.

Or, carefully drop Gow Gees into a pan of deep, hot oil, (not over hot) 8–10 at a time, and cook for 4–5 minutes, until golden brown. Lift out, drain and serve hot with Plum or Sweet and Sour Sauce.

# Plum Sauce

Cooking time: 4–5 minutes

*1 cup plum jam*
*½ cup mango chutney*
*2 tablespoons sugar*
*3 tablespoons vinegar*

Mix jam and chutney together and sieve into a pan. Stir in sugar and vinegar and heat, stirring to dissolve sugar, until sauce is hot. Serve hot or cold. Makes almost 2 cups.

# Barbecue Sauce

Cooking time: 4–5 minutes

*1 clove garlic, crushed*
*½ teaspoon salt*
*2 tablespoons honey*
*2 teaspoons vinegar*
*2 tablespoons soy sauce*
*3 tablespoons sherry*
*1 tablespoon hoi sin sauce*

Combine garlic, salt, honey, vinegar, soy sauce, sherry and hoi sin sauce in a pan and bring to the boil, stirring. Reduce heat and simmer, stirring constantly, for 2–3 minutes. Serve hot or cold. Makes a little over ⅔ cup.

# Chili Sauce

Cooking time: 4–5 minutes

  2 teaspoons sugar
  ¼ teaspoon chili powder
  2 cloves garlic, crushed
  2 slices root ginger, crushed
  1 tablespoon oil
  2 teaspoons dry sherry
  1 tablespoon soy sauce
  ¼ cup tomato catsup
  2 teaspoons Chinese chili sauce
  3 tablespoons water

Combine sugar, chili powder, garlic, ginger, oil, sherry, soy, tomato and chili sauces and water in a pan and bring to the boil, stirring, reduce heat and simmer for 2–3 minutes, stirring constantly. Serve hot or cold. Makes a little over ¾ cup.

# Lemon Sauce

Cooking time: 12–15 minutes

  ½ cup (125 ml) chicken stock
  pinch of salt
  1 piece of lemon rind
  ¼ cup lemon juice
  1 slice of root ginger, crushed
  1 tablespoon sugar
  2 teaspoons cornstarch
  1 tablespoon water

Combine chicken stock, salt, lemon rind and juice, ginger and sugar in a pan and stir over low heat, until sugar is dissolved. Bring to the boil, reduce heat, cover and simmer for 4–5 minutes, then strain into a separate pan.
Blend cornstarch with water, until smooth and stir into the sauce. Cook for 2 minutes, stirring, until sauce thickens, then reduce heat and simmer for 4–5 minutes. Serve hot or cold. Makes almost 1 cup.

# Sweet and Sour Sauce

  1½ tablespoons cornstarch
  ½ cup (125 ml) water
  2 tablespoons sugar
  2 tablespoons soy sauce
  2 tablespoons vinegar
  1½ tablespoons tomato catsup
  1½ tablespoons dry sherry

Blend cornstarch with water in a pan, stir in sugar, soy sauce, vinegar, tomato sauce and sherry and heat gently until sugar is dissolved and the sauce thickens. Makes a little over 1¼ cups.

# Seafood Sauce

  1 cup (250 ml) mayonnaise
  ¼ cup lemon juice
  2 teaspoons vinegar
  ½ cup tomato catsup
  1 teaspoon Worcestershire sauce
  1 teaspoon anchovy paste

Combine mayonnaise, lemon juice, vinegar, tomato, Worcestershire and anchovy sauces in a bowl and mix until blended. Spoon into an air-tight jar and chill. Makes about 1¾ cups.

# Caramel Sauce

Cooking time: 8–10 minutes

  1 tablespoon cornstarch
  ¼ cup milk
  1 cup brown sugar, firmly packed
  2 tablespoons butter
  2 teaspoons corn syrup
  2 teaspoons lemon juice
  ½ cup (125 ml) heavy cream

Blend cornstarch with milk in a bowl. Combine brown sugar and butter in the top of a double pan

and heat, stirring, over simmering water, until melted and smooth. Add golden syrup, lemon juice and cornstarch mixture and stir until boiling, then boil for 3 minutes. Remove from heat and cool slightly, then gradually fold in the cream to make a smooth sauce.
Serve hot or cold. Makes about 2 cups.

# Oyster Sauce

Cooking time: 4–5 minutes

*2 teaspoons cornstarch*
*1 cup (250 ml) chicken stock*
*1½ tablespoons oyster sauce*
*1 tablespoon soy sauce*
*2 teaspoons sugar*
*2 tablespoons sherry*

Blend cornstarch with stock in a pan, until smooth, gradually stir in oyster and soy sauces, sugar and sherry and bring to the boil, stirring to dissolve sugar, and cook for 1–2 minutes. Serve hot or cold. Makes almost 1½ cups.

# Peanut Sauce

Cooking time: 10–12 minutes

*1 tablespoon oil*
*2 teaspoons minced onion*
*1 clove garlic, crushed*
*¾ cup crunchy peanut butter*
*1 tablespoon soy sauce*
*1 tablespoon brown sugar*
*1 tablespoon lemon juice*
*1 teaspoon chili sauce*
*1 cup (250 ml) water, approximately*

Heat the oil in a pan, add onion and garlic and sauté until light brown, stir in peanut butter, soy sauce, brown sugar, lemon juice and chili sauce and heat, stirring. Gradually stir in water, a little at a time, until at the boil. Sauce should not be too thick or too thin. Serve hot or cold. Makes a little over 2 cups.

# Dipping Mixes and Sauces

### Soya-Sherry Dip
Combine equal quantities of soy sauce and dry sherry and mix.

### Soya-Chili Dip
Combine 2 tablespoons soy sauce with 1 tablespoon of chili sauce and mix.

### Soya-Garlic Dip
Combine 4 tablespoons of soy sauce with 2 cloves of crushed garlic and mix.

### Soya-Mustard Dip
Combine 2 tablespoons soy sauce with ½ teaspoon of prepared English mustard and mix.

### Soya-Tomato-Chili Dip
Combine 2 tablespoons of tomato sauce, 2 tablespoons soy sauce and 2 teaspoons chili sauce and mix.

### Fried Salt and Pepper Mix
Mix 3 teaspoons salt, 1 teaspoon five spice powder and ½ teaspoon pepper in a pre-heated, absolutely dry pan over low heat and cook for 1½–2 minutes.

### Black Bean and Sherry Sauce
Rinse and mash 1 tablespoon of black beans, add 3 tablespoons dry sherry, 1 teaspoon sugar and a few drops of sesame oil. Mix together and serve cold.

### Soya and Ginger Sauce
Combine 4 tablespoons soy sauce with 2 teaspoons of very finely chopped fresh ginger and a pinch of black pepper in a small pan, bring to the boil and simmer for 2 minutes.

### Vinegar and Ginger Sauce

Combine 1 tablespoon very finely chopped ginger, 1 clove garlic, crushed, 4 tablespoons vinegar, 1 teaspoon sugar, 1 teaspoon tomato paste, pinch of salt, pepper and glutamate in a bowl and mix.

### Sherry and Egg Sauce

Combine 1 lightly beaten egg, 1 tablespoon soy sauce, 1 tablespoon dry sherry and 2 teaspoons sesame oil and mix together until smooth, serve cold.

# Special Ingredients

Many ingredients used are the same as used in general cooking and are available at Supermarkets and or Health Food Stores. It may be necessary to shop at Chinese Food Stores to buy certain items, such as Hoi Sin sauce, Hoi Sin Jeong sauce, Chinese dried mushrooms, star anise etc.

**Abalone** is a shellfish with a delectable flavor, use sliced as an appetiser or in soups. Available in cans.

**Bamboo Shoots** are sometimes available fresh at Chinese Food Stores, are also sold in cans. Rinse under running water before use. Need only a short cooking time.

**Bean Sprouts** are very crunchy shoots of the mung bean. Recommend using the fresh as the canned sprouts are mushy. If canned bean sprouts are used, they should be washed and drained. Available at Chinese Food Stores and sometimes at Greengrocers.

**Bean Curd** is available in sticks and sheets at Chinese Food Stores. Soak before using.

**Black Beans** are used, mashed, to darken sauces and meat dishes. They are made from heavily salted soya beans.

**Chinese Barbecue Sauce** is sweet, salty and reddish in color. Use as a dip or in barbecue marinades.

**Chinese Brown Bean Sauce** is salty, made from soya beans, salt and flour.

**Chinese Cabbage** is known also as celery cabbage or Chinese lettuce. It has a celery cabbage flavor and is ideal in stir-fried dishes. It needs only a little cooking time.

**Chinese Chili Sauce** has a special, different flavor. Use Tabasco Sauce as a substitute, in an emergency.

**Chinese Dried Mushrooms** are grey black in color, but black are the thickest and the best. The flavor is most distinctive. Available only at Chinese Food Stores.

**Chinese Hoi Sin Sauce** is a thick, spicy, reddish-brown, pouring sauce made from salted beans, onions, garlic, sugar, salt, caramel and red rice spices.

**Chinese Satay Sauce** has a seasoned garlic, chili flavor and is available in cans or jars.

**Chinese Mixed Pickles** are a mixture of onion, melon, bell pepper, leeks and ginger.

**Chinese Plum Sauce** is a spicy, chutney, sweet, hot sauce made from chillies, vinegar, plums, sugar and spices.

**Chinese Red Powder** is used very sparingly to give a red color to some dishes.

**Five Spice Powder** gives a subtle aroma and flavor to dishes, is made from Szechuan pepper, ground star anise, fennel, cloves and cinnamon.

**Ginger** is a basic seasoning in Chinese foods, it has a sharp taste. The fresh root is the best to use and only in small amounts. Ginger Syrup is also used and this is available in bottles or cans.

**Glutamate** or more correctly, Monosodium Glutamate (Ve-Tsin in China) is a white crystalized powder extracted from grains and vegetables. It enhances the natural flavors of food. Often called Gourmet Powder.

**Sesame Oil** is a nutty aromatic oil and is used sparingly for added flavor.

**Star Anise** imparts a licorice flavor to poultry and meat dishes, or in soups, but use sparingly.

# Measurements

See chart on opposite page for imperial and metric equivalents. Some metric measurements have been listed in recipes for the convenience of those using them. Where spoon measurements are used, these indicate level spoons.

Servings are on the basis that the recipe will provide the number of servings indicated. Where more dishes are served at one meal, the number of servings will be increased, thus 2 recipes for 4 will provide sufficient food for 8 people.

Many of the dishes illustrated were prepared and photographed at THE HOUSE OF CHINA RESTAURANT, CROWS NEST, NSW, AUSTRALIA

# Liquid Measures Table

| IMPERIAL | METRIC |
|---|---|
| 1 teaspoon | 5 ml |
| *1 tablespoon (Aust) | 20 ml |
| 2 fluid ounces (¼ cup) | 65 ml |
| 4 fluid ounces (½ cup) | 125 ml |
| 8 fluid ounces (1 cup) | 250 ml |
| 1 pint (20 fluid ounces = 2½ cups) | 625 ml |

| USA | METRIC |
|---|---|
| *1 tablespoon (also UK and NZ) | 15 ml |
| 1 pint (16 ounces = 2 cups) | 500 ml |
| All other measures same as | |
| for imperial, above | |

*Tablespoon measures used in the recipes in this book are 15 ml.

# Solid Measures Table

| AVOIRDUPOIS | METRIC |
|---|---|
| 1 ounce | 30 g |
| 4 ounces (¼ lb) | 125 g |
| 8 ounces (½ lb) | 250 g |
| 12 ounces (¾ lb) | 375 g |
| 16 ounces (1 lb) | 500 g |
| 24 ounces (1½ lb) | 750 g |
| 32 ounces (2 lb) | 1000 g (1 kg) |

# Oven Temperature Table

| DESCRIPTION | GAS | | ELECTRIC | | DIAL MARK |
|---|---|---|---|---|---|
| | C | F | C | F | |
| Cool | 100 | 200 | 110 | 225 | ¼ |
| Very slow | 120 | 250 | 120 | 250 | ½ |
| Slow | 150 | 300 | 150 | 300 | 1–2 |
| Moderately slow | 160 | 325 | 170 | 340 | 3 |
| Moderate | 180 | 350 | 190 | 375 | 4 |
| Moderately hot | 190 | 375 | 220 | 425 | 5–6 |
| Hot | 200 | 400 | 250 | 475 | 6–7 |
| Very hot | 230 | 450 | 270 | 525 | 8–9 |

# Index

# Notes